$25   27462

D1055669

DATE DUE

The Ancient Dialect

The Ancient Dialect

Thomas Carlyle and Comparative Religion

Ruth apRoberts

University of California Press

Berkeley / Los Angeles / London

University of California Press
Berkeley and Los Angeles, California

University of California Press, Ltd.
London, England

Library of Congress Cataloging-in-Publication Data

ApRoberts, Ruth
  The ancient dialect.
  Includes index.
    1. Religion—Study and teaching—England—History—
19th Century. 2. Carlyle, Thomas, 1795-1881—Views
on comparative religion. I.Title.
BL41.A67   1988   291'.092'4   87-19062

Printed in the United States of America

1 2 3 4 5 6 7 8 9

I owe much to the scholarship and kindness of three distinguished
Carlyleans: Ian Campbell, K. J. Fielding, and Georg B. Tennyson. They have my warm thanks.

Contents

A Note on Sources

The frequently used editions of Carlyle's works are cited in the notes by the following short titles:

Essays	*Critical and Miscellaneous Essays.* Volumes 26–30 of *The Works of Thomas Carlyle.* Edinburgh Edition. New York: Charles Scribner's Sons, 1903.
Heroes, Works	*Heroes and Hero-Worship.* Volume 5 of *The Works of Thomas Carlyle.*
Sartor	*Sartor Resartus.* Edited by C. F. Harrold. New York: The Odyssey Press, Inc., 1939; Indianapolis: Bobbs-Merrill, 1979.
Letters	*The Collected Letters of Thomas and Jane Welsh Carlyle.* Duke-Edinburgh Edition. 12 volumes. Edited by C. R. Sanders, Kenneth J. Fielding, et al. Durham: Duke University Press, 1970–1985.

All translations of foreign languages are my own, unless specified otherwise.

1. "The Poet at the Beginning of Days"

Dorothea Brooke, the Saint Theresa of *Middlemarch*, in love with religion and with learning, yearns for some "binding theory which could bring her own life and doctrine into strict . . . connection with . . . the amazing past." She has encountered surprisingly impressive religions of past ages, and the problem is how to adjust her devout spirit to a multi-religioned history of mankind when she has been brought up to accept Christianity as the One Way. She marries the dryasdust Mr. Casaubon in the faith that she may assist him in his great learned project, "The Key to All the Mythologies," which she understands will address this very problem. The course of her sad disillusionment makes one of the most memorable stories in Victorian fiction. She is overqualified for the work; she innocently perseveres in selfless research assistance, to discover at last that her husband is pathetically inadequate and misguided.

What is Casaubon's line of research? Dr. Johnson had declared that the business of philosophy and literature was to discover the Great General Truths, which are to be discerned beneath the superficies of different times and places. His *Rasselas* takes place in Africa, but his hero is as un-African as Everyman, and the adventures and ideas are devoid of local color. His Africa is only a device to distance and demonstrate the ubiquitous and unchanging nature of the human condition. But the new science emanating from Germany in Dorothea's time set itself squarely against any static general "Truth" of human nature. The Germans insisted on the diversity and uniqueness of cultures; it now seemed that a human being is shaped by his particular society, its language, its art, its religion. Historicism urged the study of the differences, especially in that all-engrossing, life-and-death matter of religion. Multiplicity and diversity of religions in history make a problem for the orthodox worldview. Where does

Christianity fit in among these diversities? How can we find a "binding theory" that will bring our lives and Christian doctrine into a relation with this "amazing past"? This pressing inquiry led ultimately to a new school of developmental theology and the Higher Criticism of the Bible, but in early phases it elicited some desperate devices, such as a reactionary, pseudo-scientific "Mythography," which held that primitive and pagan religions represented corruptions of the original, single, divine revelation and that all languages are derived from the original Hebrew, lost in the famous incident at the Tower of Babel.[1]

This was the orthodoxy that Casaubon aimed to support with his massive project, "The Key to All the Mythologies." The theory depended on the most naive biblical literalism and required the researcher to stretch and finagle his evidence; it developed a wildly lunatic fringe of Druids and lost Atlantises and British Israelitism. One imagines that Blake's heated declaration that "all religions are one!" has some connection with this school. Meanwhile, responsible German scholarship was making advances in the study of the languages, the history, and the cultures of the Near East, with a great school of Orientalists. And Casaubon, as his cousin Will Ladislaw points out, is no Orientalist; he doesn't even know German. George Eliot knew, and Ladislaw knew, that Karl Otfried Müller had published a *Prolegomena to a Scientific Study of Mythology* in 1825, which exploded the whole "Mythography" enterprise. Müller exposes the absurdity of Casaubon-style etymological "proofs" relating various myths to a Hebrew origin and demonstrates that mythologies develop independently. Casaubon is a hopeless anachronism—retrogressive, futile, and doomed.

Dorothea should have met Thomas Carlyle, her contemporary. George Eliot is writing *Middlemarch* in 1870, looking back on the period before the first Reform Bill of 1832; Dorothea's crisis is contemporary with Carlyle's. In a way, she does meet Carlyle—for Will Ladislaw embodies the new German learning that Carlyle was to import and domesticate in England. Casaubon recognizes it in his negative way when he deplores Will's choice of Heidelberg rather than

1. See Vernon Storr, *The Development of English Theology in the Nineteenth Century* (London, 1913), pp. 179, 296. See W. J. Harvey's excellent study of Casaubon's research interest, "The Intellectual Background of the Novel: Casaubon and Lydgate," in *Middlemarch: Critical Approaches to the Novel*, ed. B. Hardy (London: The Athlone Press; New York: Oxford University Press, 1967), pp. 25–37.

an English university and protests his determination to go abroad
again, "without any special object, save the vague purpose of what he
calls culture" (chap. 9). Carlyle explains: "The great law of culture is:
Let each become all that he was created capable of being; expand, if
possible, to his full growth."[2] Culture, for both George Eliot and
Carlyle, is the great German principle of *Bildung*, and it is a Goethean
ideal. It forbids us to constrict the mind with any dogma; it invites us
to embrace the whole of recorded human experience. Since religion—
for Dorothea, for Carlyle—is the most important part of that experience, it is incumbent on us to come to terms with the varieties of
religions, and we need a method to bring ourselves into relation with
"the amazing past." Or, as Carlyle puts it, man who looks before and
after "would fain unite himself in clear, conscious relation, with the
whole Future and the whole Past."[3] Casaubon's method cripples the
intellect and defeats itself. Carlyle borrows the method of the Germans to become the pioneer of Comparative Religion in England.

It is one mark of Carlyle's method that he repeatedly speaks of
poetry and religion as though they were much the same thing. This
comes out of the German Historicism that derives—chiefly—from
Johann Gottfried von Herder and encompasses Comparative Philology, Comparative Religion, and the Higher Criticism of the Bible. In
contradistinction to Johnsonian General Truths, Herder in his *Ideen
zur Philosophie der Geschichte der Menschheit* (1784–1791) envisions the infinite variety of civilizations in the vastness of space and of
time and insists on the uniqueness of each society, which exists in its
own terms and is to be judged by its own standards and valued as its
own unique variety or phase of human development. (Herder can be
said to have invented cultural anthropology in fact—though the palm
sometimes goes to Vico, or Comte, or Durkheim.) For Herder,
moreover, each society goes through a cycle of *Entwicklung*, development. In the early phase, man sees his surroundings as manipulated
by spirits, gods—that is, he sees anthropomorphically and sees, even
"makes," his distinctive world with his anthropomorphic metaphors,
woven together into patterns of myth. These are by no means to be
dismissed as mere outworn savagery; they constitute, rather, the world
by which a society lives; they are society's most important, precious,
and distinctively human creations. Myth, and the metaphors that

2. "Jean Paul Friedrich Richter" (1827), *Essays* 1:19.
3. "On History," *Essays* 2:83.

make up myth, represent in the accessible form of images the felt relations of man to creation and to his society—relations otherwise hardly to be explained. The way of metaphor, of image, is the *human* way, as Hamann had said before Herder: "Sinne und Leidenschaften reden und verstehen nur als Bilder"—"Perception and passion speak and understand by images alone."[4] In the early phases of a culture, these images—metaphors or myths—are understood literally: Jupiter really does throw thunderbolts, an anthropomorphic God really does walk in the cool of the evening in Eden. Later phases of a culture will continue to value the myth but will understand the unscientific unbelievable husk of the story as an embodiment of essential meaning. Man functions more by his senses than by his reason; Lessing, typically, construes the account of Eden: "The source of moral evil, too abstract a truth for a sensual people to understand, is bodied forth in the story of a forbidden tree."

If metaphor is the stuff of poetry, as it is traditionally taken to be, then the early mythmakers, religionists, are quite conveniently to be called poets. And indeed the etymology of *poet* in Greek, and *maker* in English, bears out this expressionist sense. Our own Sir Philip Sidney in a notable passage explains the poet-maker as participating in the power of his "heavenly Maker": "With the force of a divine breath he bringeth things forth." The German Hamann even calls God Himself "the Poet at the beginning of days"—God making us a world of symbols in which to read our spiritual meanings. Emerson accordingly finds Nature a vast repository of analogues and metaphors; and for Carlyle, man "everywhere finds himself encompassed with Symbols, recognized as such or not recognized." Carlyle at times when he sounds orthodox, such as when he speaks of God, says he is using the "ancient dialect."[5] It is his way of saying that he is borrowing the metaphorical mode of the early mythmaker, and that he, Carlyle, does not mean a literal God, though the early man did. The phrase does much more: it safeguards his honesty; it obscures his rationalism enough to protect the feelings of pious literalists; at the same time it suggests the genuine veneration he has for the "poets at the beginning of days." It does all this with the sublime concision and resonance

4. *Aesthetica in Nuce*, quoted in James C. O'Flaherty, "Languages and Reason in the Thought of Hamann," in *Creative Encounter: Festschrift for Herman Salinger*, ed. L. R. Phelps (Chapel Hill: Univ. of North Carolina Press, 1978), p. 88.

5. For example, in *Past and Present*, *Works* 10:136.

characteristic of *this* poet, Carlyle the master of metaphor. According to Herderian theory, the pre-Homeric Greeks, the Old Testament Jews, the early *Volk* of northern Europe were all poets, mythmakers. *Das Volk dichtet*, said the Germans. Matthew Arnold echoes the idea when he speaks of the writing of the Old Testament books: *Israel was a poet*. Carlyle quotes Goethe: "Who but the Poet was it that first formed gods for us; that exalted us to them, and brought them down to us!"[6]

This line of thinking, with its Herderian cultural relativism, is obviously heterodox. Herder implied that all cultures are equal in the eye of God, and *this* has the shocking implication that all religions may be equally valid. The Judeo-Christian tradition is no longer privileged; it is one religion or—to say it more boldly—one myth among others. This is the radical essence of the Higher Criticism. It develops in two lines: one line is the reductionists, like F. C. Baur, who say the whole thing is *mere* myth; the other line is the reverential Mythological School represented by Schleiermacher, who rejects all supernaturalism but finds the myth infinitely precious. His *reverence* is the basis of Carlyle's *wonder*, the religion of Natural Supernaturalism.

And so it is that Carlyle in his pivotal essay "The State of German Literature" (1827) ends on what was for him the central point of the whole German school:

> To the charge of Irreligion . . . the Germans will plead not guilty. On the contrary, they will not scruple to assert that their literature is, in a positive sense, religious; nay, perhaps to maintain, that if ever neighbouring nations are to recover that pure and high spirit of devotion . . . it must be by travelling, if not on the same path, at least in the same direction in which the Germans have already begun to travel.[7]

6. See *Carlyle's Unfinished History of German Literature*, ed. Hill Shine (Lexington: Univ. of Kentucky Press, 1951), p. 3. David DeLaura studies the Victorian religion-aesthetics problem but seems unaware of this essential understanding of "poetry" as mythmaking or religion-making ("The Future of Poetry: A Context for Carlyle and Arnold," in *Carlyle and His Contemporaries: Essays in Honor of Charles Richard Sanders*, ed. John Clubbe [Durham: Duke Univ. Press, 1976], pp. 148–80). DeLaura forgets how concerned both Carlyle and Arnold were with the literature of the Bible. For Carlyle, the Psalms and the Book of Job were quintessential poetry; for Arnold it was these plus especially the Book of Isaiah. "Isaiah is immensely superior to Milton's *Comus* . . . even as literature" (see my *Arnold and God* [Berkeley: Univ. of California Press, 1983], p. 245).

7. *Essays* 1:84–85.

And now he makes the point-blank equivalence: "Religion, Poetry, is not dead; it will never die."[8] Note that he is not speaking of two entities; the thing, Religion-Poetry, is single. In "Characteristics" (1831) he is more specific: "Literature is but a branch of Religion, and always participates in its character; however, in our time, it is the only branch that still shows any greenness; and, as some think, must one day become the main stem."[9] More frankly yet, he writes in a letter to Goethe, "Literature is now nearly all in all to us; not our speech only, but our Worship and Lawgiving; our best Priest must henceforth be our Poet; the *Vates* will in future be practically all that he ever was in theory."[10]

One of Carlyle's German studies was his 1828 essay on Zacharias Werner, a dramatist now little known or regarded who seems to have lived and breathed the subject of religion, from his most popular hit, *Martin Luther oder die Weihe der Kraft* (Martin Luther or the consecration of power), to his death as a devoted convert to Roman Catholicism. It is from Werner's peculiar works on the Knights Templar, wherein are deployed Rosicrucianism, Masonic rites, and other hermetic and spooky matters, that Carlyle gets the peculiar word *Baphometic* he used in *Sartor*. Out of all the welter of Werner's religious interests, Carlyle turns in the conclusion of this essay to the central issue.

> It is a common theory among the Germans, that every Creed, every Form of worship, is a *form* merely; the mortal and ever changing *body*, in which the immortal and unchanging *spirit* of Religion is, with more or less completeness, expressed to the material eye, and made manifest and influential among the doings of men. . . . Johannes Müller, in his *Universal History*, professes to consider the Mosaic Law, the creed of Mahomet, nay Luther's Reformation; and in short, all other systems of Faith . . . without special praise or censure, simply as *Vorstellungsarten*, "Modes of Representation."[11]

Carlyle is recognizing the new phenomenon of Comparative Religion, and the flower of this line of thinking is the great metaphor of clothes for *Vorstellungsarten*, and *Sartor Resartus* itself. His most specifically comparative-religious subjects, however, are the first two lectures of

8. *Essays* 1:85–86.
9. *Essays* 3:23.
10. *Letters* 5:220.
11. *Essays* 1:143–44.

Heroes and Hero-Worship, "The Hero as Divinity"—Odin; and "The Hero as Prophet"—Mahomet. Critics of *Heroes* and Carlyle's concept of the hero have passed over these rather lightly, getting on with "The Hero as Poet"—Dante and Shakespeare; "The Hero as Priest"—Luther and Knox; "The Hero as Man of Letters"—Johnson, Rousseau, Burns; and "The Hero as King"—Cromwell and Napoleon. But the first two are essential to the logic of the series; they make particularly clear some of Carlyle's essential thinking; and perhaps better than any other text they reveal Carlyle as the practitioner of Comparative Religion. They invite the closest consideration. First, we need to look at their provenance: how did Carlyle arrive at the subjects of Odin and Mahomet in the peculiar perspective of *Heroes and Hero-Worship?*

2. Counter-Enlightenment: Hume to Goethe

Sartor Resartus is one of the landmark texts of modern times, signaling as it does what can be thought of as the basic change in cultural perspective from the Single and Absolute to the many and relative; from the Great General Truth of the Enlightenment to the many and variable, the perpetually shifting, the multifarious; from one Truth to an ever-expanding pluralism; from dogma to an infinite series of hypotheses. Carlyle's metaphor of clothes is beautifully adapted and beautifully exploited to usher in this vertiginous cultural shift. For Carlyle, despite all his figurative demurrers, the central issue is religious—that is what makes it a matter of life and death. And he sees that the shift must be away from the old oneness of European Christendom, which had occasioned so many wars of religion fought over *which* oneness was to be supreme, toward a pluralism of Christianities and, still further in the expanding purview of the historicist imagination, toward a realization of the validity of religions other than Christianity. This is the impulse that lies behind the *Heroes* lectures on Odin and Mahomet. They extend the pluralism of *Sartor* specifically into the field of religion.

Carlyle's great countryman David Hume had been the prophet of comparativism; "ironic" Hume played an oddly ironic part in the history of the study of religion. He appears to represent supremely the rationalism of the French Enlightenment, with its permanent unalterable structures working by universal and unchanging laws, all discernible by reason and science; but the very scrupulousness of his rationalism led to an odd turn in this matter of religion.[1] He aimed from the first "To Introduce the Experimental Method of Reasoning

1. On Hume and Hamann, I draw from Isaiah Berlin's "Hume and the Sources of German Anti-Rationalism" (1977), reprinted in *Against the Current* (New York: Viking Press, 1980), pp. 162–87.

into Moral Subjects"[2] and accordingly produced *The Natural History of Religion* (1757), the term "Natural History" being the equivalent of our *science*.

The typical Enlightenment Deist attitude had been to assume that of course since Christianity was true, all rational processes would prove it so, and the Deists posited a generalized monotheism clean of supernatural or superstitious elements; they considered it consonant with the tenets of the Anglican church, and they declared it to be "natural religion," something that humankind in all places and times will "naturally" turn to. But Hume was simply too enlightened by reason to underwrite the Deists. His rational skepticism extended to epistemology itself. "Our existence," he says, "and the existence of other things must be believed and cannot be demonstrated."[3] How little, then, can any "truth" of Christianity or of any other religion be demonstrated! He attacks the Deist idea of "natural religion" as utterly without basis; polytheism, according to the evidence, must be the earliest form of religion as well as the most "natural." He considers all religions to be as superstitious and as false as polytheism, and he particularly castigates the superstitions of Christianity. Christianity was from the first, he comments dryly in a famous passage, attended by miracles; and so it is now too—whenever anyone believes in it. "And whoever is moved by *Faith* to assent to it, is conscious of a continued miracle in his own person, which subverts all the principles of his understanding, and gives him a determination to believe what is most contrary to custom and experience."[4]

One of Carlyle's challenges was to come to terms with Hume. In "Signs of the Times" Carlyle acclaims him for seeing that in these days "Religion must have a Natural History"; that is, we must at last develop a science of religion. But Hume's values are all wrong. Hume "regards [Religion] as a Disease, we again as Health; so far there is a difference; but in our first principle we are at one."[5] The humane Carlyle recognizes this capacity for religion as part of the distinguishing quality of mankind. Conscious of the great saints and doctors before us, of Luther and Calvin and such a poet as Dante, how can we call it a disease! The study of this human capacity for religion is to Carlyle an urgent and timely challenge to the scientific intellect.

2. The phrase is the subtitle of his *Treatise on Human Nature* (1739).
3. Quoted by Berlin, p. 180.
4. Hume's *Enquiries*, quoted by Berlin, p. 177.
5. *Essays* 2:76.

Hume was early translated and widely read in Germany and had a marked influence on German epistemology. He had an especially interesting effect on the religious thought of Johann Georg Hamann, "The Magus of the North" (1730–1788), whom we have much reason to love, for his originality and wit, for his importance to Nietzsche and Kierkegaard, for his endearing metaphors of sexuality—"The abstractions of the rationalists are the *castration* of knowledge"[6]—for his appreciation of the power of metaphor itself, and for his flashing insight into the fictive character of language. Originally from a pietist background, he became a promising young light of the *Aufklärung*. A violent spiritual crisis, however, revealed the inadequacies and vanities of rationalism to him. The pietist Count Zinzendorf, leader of the Herrnhuter brethren, or Moravians, had declared, "Whoever seeks to conceive God in his head becomes an atheist." Now Hamann joined the pietists in deploring French rationalistic materialism and atheism. For Hamann, the only valid convictions—or acts or words—involve the whole man, who is whole only in his mystical response to the Logos. For him, "in Paris the monstrous *cogito* has obscured the divine *sum*."[7] Hamann's rational friends made an effort to save him from this new obscurantism; no less a person than Kant was set on him to re-enlighten him. But this was as nothing to Hamann, too polite to dismiss his friend Kant but privately convinced that Kant moved in darkness, the darkness of his unreal faculty psychology and his ignorance of the role language plays in cognition.

Hamann considered Hume his philosophical ally and did a translation of Hume's posthumous *Dialogues Concerning Natural Religion*. As Isaiah Berlin writes, Hamann's interest in Hume was intense but narrow, confined to Hume's views on the limits of reason, but that was enough. Hamann writes that Hume is "a spirit for tearing down, not building up, that is indeed his glory"[8]—it was in just these terms that Carlyle was to evaluate other heroes of the Enlightenment: Diderot and Voltaire. And so Hamann embraces Hume's view of the limits of reason and uses it to revalidate the irrational, rejoicing to find truth in the mouth of an unbeliever. He turns Hume's epistemology about, to glorify the mystery of being, "the divine *sum*." For Hamann truth is always particular, in the immediate experience of an image,

6. Berlin, p. 170.
7. Berlin, p. 169.
8. Berlin, p. 175.

never general, as in dogma; God is a poet, not a mathematician. He especially rejoices in Hume's ironic statement on Christian miracles and delights to de-ironize it: of *course*, it is a miracle to believe in Christianity. "What is there in nature that is not a miracle for us?"[9] Anyone familiar with Carlyle's religion of Wonder will see its prototype in Hamann. It is as though it was something conceived by Hamann out of Hume. One would be inclined to search the evidence for Carlyle's close reading of Hamann, though all we have on the surface is Carlyle's occasional mention of him. But then Hamann himself is considered the father of that energizing *Sturm und Drang* movement and had particular effect on Jacobi, Herder, and Goethe, all of whom would mediate the Hamannian Counter-Enlightenment to Carlyle.

The more sober German line of *Religionswissenschaft* of Gotthold Ephraim Lessing (1729–1781) was well known to Carlyle. Lessing distinguished himself both from orthodox Christianity and from rationalist skepticism by a respect for religious phenomena as such and by an objectivity in treating them. He published the *Wolfenbüttel Fragments* (1774–1778), Reimarus's sensational attack on miracles and biblical inerrancy and a landmark of the Higher Criticism; he himself wrote "The Evangelists Regarded as Merely Human Historians" (1778); and most important of all, in *Die Erziehung des Menschengeschlechts* (The education of the human race) (1780), he put forward historical development as the rule in religion as in other things. For him, no dogmatic creed can be regarded as final; every historical religion makes a contribution to mankind's spiritual development. The French developed these ideas into Saint-Simonianism and Comtism; Carlyle owned a copy of *Die Erziehung* in a French translation of 1830.[10] Heine, that valiant German soldier in humanity's war of liberation, took up his mission in Paris, the city of light and capital of Liberty, and he viewed Lessing from there as "the second great liberator."[11] Just as Luther freed us from the tyranny of Roman Catholicism, so Lessing frees us from the tyranny of biblical

---

9. Berlin, p. 178.
10. See K. J. Fielding, "Carlyle and the Saint-Simonians (1830–1832): New Considerations," in *Carlyle and His Contemporaries: Essays in Honor of Charles Richard Sanders*, ed. John Clubbe (Durham: Duke Univ. Press, 1976), p. 39.
11. Carlyle revered Lessing but had little respect for Heine: "Blackguard Heine is worth very little" (*Letters* 9:85).

literalism, as the hull or husk of Christianity falls away to reveal and free the spirit, the *Geist* of it.[12] Lessing had declared, Heine proclaims, against the constriction of what Coleridge was to call bibliolatry.

Lessing was also a playwright, and his play *Nathan der Weise* (1779) was famous and available in French and English translations from the first.[13] In a list of German books for Jane about 1821, Carlyle recommends *Nathan* as "easy and good"; he is still recommending it in 1834, to Jeffrey. And in a letter of 1826 Jane refers to "the last oracle of Nathan's."[14] The "oracle" must be that famous Fable of the Three Rings. Lessing felt the play to be the crown of his career, and in a way the fable itself is the essence of the play's poignant plea for tolerance, the wise Nathan being modeled on Lessing's brilliant and saintly friend Moses Mendelssohn. The fable will serve us, I think, as a *Bild*, or image, of the comparative idea. The play, which takes place in Jerusalem, exhibits Christians, Moslems, and Jews: Saladin has asked the wise Jew Nathan which of the three great religions is the true one. Nathan promises an answer, and Saladin asks when they are at last alone, "Now tell me—No one can hear us." Nathan answers, "It would be well if the whole world heard us."

A great deal of the world did hear the story that Nathan proceeds to tell: There was once a man who possessed a wonderful ring that made its owner beloved of God and man. As he grew old, he was troubled to decide which one of his three equally beloved sons should inherit the ring. He called in a jeweler and ordered two exact replicas of it—and the jeweler succeeded so well that even the owner could not tell the rings apart. When in due course the man came to die, each son received a ring and each thought he had the original. Lessing got the story from Boccaccio and developed it in this religious sense with great wit and delicacy. The point is, of course, that whether you are Moslem or Jew or Christian, you had better respect your two brothers, for one of them may have the *real* thing. Hereby was

---

12. "Nachdem Luther uns von der Tradizion befreyt, und die Bibel zur alleinigen Quelle des Christenthums erhoben hatte, da enstand . . . ein starrer Wortdienst, und der Buchstabe der Bibel herrschte eben so tyrannisch wie einst die Tradizion. Zur Befreyung von diesem tyrannischen Buchstaben hat nun Lessing am meisten beygetragen" (*Heine über Lessing, 1834* [Weimar: Nationale Forschungs- und Gedenkstätten der klassischen deutschen Literatur, 1980], p. 3).

13. See Wilhelm Todt, *Lessing in England, 1767–1850* (Heidelberg: Carl Winters Universitätsbuchhandlung, 1912).

14. *Letters* 4:55, 9:390.

inculcated, for many, an eloquent lesson against Christian provincialism.[15]

Nathan der Weise is a classic statement of religious tolerance; it was still felt to be timely on 7 September 1945, when it was the play chosen for the reopening of the Berliner Deutsche Theater. Thomas Mann called it a force for peace.[16] Carlyle praises Lessing as a critic, controversialist, stylist, poet, dramatist; moreover, "his Criticism and philosophic or religious Scepticism were of a higher mood than had yet been heard in Europe."[17] And he observes that while writers like Wieland and Klopstock have faded, Lessing still "towers, . . . standing on the confines of Light and Darkness, like Day on the misty mountain-tops."[18]

The effect of Kant on religious thought has been enormous yet incalculable, and the question of Kant in England is vexed in the cases of Coleridge and Carlyle both, Coleridge for his dissimulations and Carlyle for his ambivalences. The specialist on the Kant question, René Wellek, has declared of Carlyle: "With his usual candor in such things—so strikingly different from Coleridge's real or sometimes pretended omniscience, he admits" that he does not altogether understand Kant.[19] Wellek traces some of Carlyle's *mis*understandings: confusion of *subjective* with *objective*, of *Verstand/Vernunft* with *head/heart*, inconsistent treatment of the Space-Time doctrine. C. F. Harrold argues that Kant was generally interpreted loosely anyway and that Carlyle owes more to Coleridge and Jacobi than to Kant.[20] Wilhelm Dilthey, however, cultural historian and himself an editor of Kant, believes that though Carlyle got his Kant mostly through Schiller, he nevertheless had a just sense of Kant's significance. "The

15. Friedrich Meinecke reminds us of the limits of Lessing's comparativism: his Nathan is not individualized but an Enlightenment generalized ideal, "'the good man' whether he be Christian, Jew or Muslim" (*Historism*, trans. J. E. Anderson [London: Routledge and Kegan Paul, 1972], p. 238).

16. Quoted in *Gotthold Ephraim Lessing: Nathan der Weise: Drei Kupferstriche aus dem Theater-Kalender auf das Jahr 1780*, Text von Konrad Kratzsch (Weimar: Nationale Forschungs- und Gedenkstätten der klassischen deutschen Literatur, 1978), p. 4.

17. "The State of German Literature," *Essays* 1:48.

18. *Essays* 2:362.

19. *Immanuel Kant in England* (Princeton: Princeton Univ. Press, 1931), p. 185. See "State of German Literature," *Essays* 1:78. This essay and the one on Novalis include Carlyle's comment on Kant.

20. *Carlyle and German Thought: 1819–1834* (1934; reprint, London: Anchor Books, 1963), p. 147.

course of thought is since Kant not from outer to inner [as with the British sensationalists] but from inner to outer." Dilthey recognizes that to Carlyle, Kant's transcendentalism was the greatest achievement of the century, comparable in magnitude only to the Reformation.[21] As Nelson Goodman sees it, "the mainstream of modern philosophy . . . began when Kant exchanged the structure of the world for the structure of the mind."[22] This essential Kant I believe Carlyle apprehended, as when he says,

> Not because Heaven existed, did men know Good from Evil; the "because," I invite you to consider, lay quite the other way. It was *because* men, having hearts as well as stomachs, felt there, and knew through all their being, the difference between God and Evil, that Heaven and Hell first came to exist. That is the sequence.[23]

This, I think, is Carlyle's stance on religious matters; it is from 1850, and he is being more frank than in his earlier works. It represents a thoroughgoing expressivist view that man makes his God and that religion is no less to be revered for this. It is what Dilthey means by "inner to outer." It is a strain of thought that leads to William James and the psychology of religion.

Where Carlyle fails to deal adequately with Kant, the reason may well be that he did not care to persist in his study, repelled for just those reasons that repelled Hamann and Herder in turn. Hamann declared that men like Kant "provide us with endless verbal constructions—words that are taken for concepts, and worse still, concepts that are taken for real things."[24] He composed a "Metakritik" that questioned whether *Vernunft* can ever be *rein*, whether reason can ever be pure, in any useful sense. Herder wrote a more extensive "Metakritik" with some telling arguments against Kant's systematic logic and his faculty psychology. Finally, Froude tells us how Carlyle, at the time of his marriage, took up *Die Kritik der reinen Vernunft* and read to page 150, whereupon he decided that "Scott's novels would answer better."[25]

Friedrich Max Müller brought over into England the whole com-

21. Wilhelm Dilthey, "Thomas Carlyle," *Archiv für Geschichte der Philosophie* 4 (1891): 264, 267.

22. *Ways of Worldmaking* (Indianapolis: Hackett Publishing Co., 1978), p. x.

23. "Jesuitism," no. 8 of *Latter-Day Pamphlets*, *Works* 20:334.

24. Quoted in *Against the Current*, p. 8.

25. J. A. Froude, *Thomas Carlyle: A History of the First Forty Years of His Life*, 2 vols. (New York: Charles Scribner's Sons, 1882; St. Clair Shores, Mich.: Scholarly Press, 1970), 1:295.

plex of German learning; besides his great edition of the *Rig Veda* and his *History of Ancient Sanskrit Literature* and his fifty-one volumes of translations of *The Sacred Books of the East*, he also published *The Science of Language* (1861–1863).[26] In the German Herderian tradition, Max Müller sees it as the mark of humanity that men are born with a capacity for language, for art, and for religion, and these capacities are not mutually exclusive. The "science" of language was felt to be a model for other fields (as indeed it has been considered again in the course of Structuralism, from Saussure the linguist through Lévi-Strauss the anthropologist).[27] Max Müller, then, as a continuation of his philology, turned to write the *Introduction to the Science of Religion* (1873), which is generally considered to have instituted the discipline of Comparative Religion.[28] This prodigious and amiable man (he remains a hero to scholarship, although his use of evidence does not quite meet our standards now) also did a translation of Kant into English. The translator's preface is full of interest and charm:

> Having once learnt from Kant what man can and what he cannot know, my plan of life was very simple, namely, to learn, so far as literature, tradition, and language allow us to do so, how man came to believe that he could know so much more than he can ever know in religion, in mythology, and in philosophy. . . . [Problems,] as Kant so often tells us, are all the making of reason, and what reason has made, reason is able to unmake. These problems represent in fact the mythology of philosophy, that is, the influence of dying or dead language on the living thought of each successive age. . . . What remains to be done, even after Kant, is to show how man came to believe that he could know so much more than he can know, and this will have to be shown by a Critique of Language. . . . How strange it is that Kant's great contemporary, "The Magus of the North," [Hamann] should have seen this at once. . . . "Language," Hamann writes, "is not only the foundation for the whole faculty of thinking, but the central point also from which proceeds the misunderstanding of reason by herself."[29]

26. See Nirad C. Chaudhuri, *Scholar Extraordinary: The Life of . . . Friedrich Max Müller* (London: Chatto and Windus, 1974).

27. See J. W. Burrow, "The Uses of Philology in Victorian England," in *Ideas and Institutions of Victorian Britain: Essays in Honour of George Kitson Clark*, ed. Robert Robson (New York: Barnes and Noble, 1967), pp. 180–204. This essay has a good discussion of Max Müller. On the "model" question, Burrow notes: "Even Darwin found comparative philology a useful analogue" (p. 188).

28. See, for instance, Eric J. Sharpe, *Comparative Religion: A History* (London: Duckworth, 1975), especially pp. 35–46.

29. *Immanuel Kant's Critique of Pure Reason*, trans. Friedrich Max Müller (1881; New York: Macmillan, 1902), pp. xxxiv–xlviii.

In a sense, I think Carlyle managed to profit enough from Kant to stand somewhat as Max Müller did in youth, with a somewhat similar "simple plan." And similarly we can profit by what Max Müller in his Germanic way calls the "dialectical evolution of thought" that ensues upon Kant:[30] Fichte, Schelling, Hegel; Coleridge and Carlyle in their ways too; Max Müller himself and a man he mentions as already a distinguished Kantian, Hans Vaihinger.[31] Max Müller appreciates Carlyle. "Mr. Carlyle had seen very deep into the very heart of mythology,"[32] he says, apropos of tracing a theme through Indian scriptures; he seems to be remembering Carlyle on the tree Igdrasil in *Heroes*. But perhaps he would have thought also that Carlyle saw deeply into the "mythology of philosophy." Where Coleridge tends to consider *Verstand* and *Vernunft* as really and absolutely distinguished, Carlyle takes them as fictions, useful enough—in fact he used them—but no more than "mythology."

Carlyle reveres Goethe beyond all others as his teacher in religious matters, but Herder might well be accounted the greatest single influence, for Carlyle appropriates Herder directly, and indirectly as well, through Goethe. The Herderian Historicism that makes the structure and message of *Sartor Resartus* is itself an idea of development in its religious dimensions.[33] Herder's key notions are basic to Carlyle's: his anthropological view of man as realizing himself only in a particular culture with its language, religion, and tradition ("It is in Society that man first feels what he is; first becomes what he can be");[34] his expressionism, the notion that man makes his culture by his language, religion, and art ("It was because men felt the difference between Good and Evil that Heaven and Hell first came to exist");[35] and his pluralism, or recognition of a potentially infinite variety of cultures, all autonomous and incommensurable with one another, succeeding each other in constant change (as of *clothes*). Herder is

30. *Kant's Critique*, p. xxxviii.
31. *Kant's Critique*, p. lxi.
32. Friedrich Max Müller, "Comparative Mythology" (1856), *Chips From a German Workshop*, vol. 2 of *Essays on Mythology Traditions and Customs* (London: Longmans, 1868), p. 130.
33. For the thought and influence of Herder, see Isaiah Berlin's important *Vico and Herder: Two Studies in the History of Ideas* (London: Hogarth Press, 1976). See also Berlin's *Against the Current*. Carlyle's debt to Herder is demonstrated and documented in Hill Shine's "Carlyle's Early Writings and Herder's *Ideen*," *Booker Memorial Studies*, ed. Hill Shine (Chapel Hill: Univ. of North Carolina Press, 1950), pp. 3–33.
34. "Characteristics," *Essays* 3:10.
35. "Jesuitism," no. 8 of *Latter-Day Pamphlets, Works* 20:334.

full, too, of a guarded religious idiom, a sense of wonder and awe in the face of biology and history; he sees the *Spur*, the trace, of the "great Being, the invisible higher Genius of humankind" in the marvelous particularities and plenitude of history, of man's arts and religions.[36] From Herder too comes Carlyle's sense of the development (*Entwicklung*) of humanity as infinite, and likewise of the individual's infinite capacities (*Bildung*).

We may trace Carlyle's gradual appropriation of Herder in his Note Books, with his emphasis on the religious issue. In 1822, musing on Milton's epistemology, he realizes that solipsism is inescapable and makes our "reasonings artificial processes," everthing varying according to our varying perceptions. "How is this?" he writes; "Truth immer WIRD nie IST?"[37]—Truth is not an absolute thing but always a *becoming*, a process, not a *being*? The statement is from Schiller.[38] It is, however, an essential concept of Herderian-Schillerian-Goethean Weimar humanism, the principle of *Entwicklung-Bildung*, that all things are in flux, even "truth," and it connotes the relativism that was so challenging to Carlyle's Scotch absolutist Calvinism, and challenging also to French universalism. This moment of "immer *wird*" might be seen as a cultural confrontation and a turning point.

Presumably soon thereafter he resolves to read "these German critics. . . . Herder I have some good hopes of." And he transcribes two lengthy passages, about five hundred words in all.[39] He refers to Herder's idea that "the notion of the soul was first suggested by the phenomena of dreams" and then transcribes, translating, the passage on sleep and death. I quote some of this, for it is typical of Herder's combination of intellectual rigor with a reverential figurative way of talking about God:

> Beautiful allegory which the Former [Maker] of our nature, by the alternation of light and darkness of sleeping and waking, has placed in the feelings of the most unthinking man! It seems as if He had wanted to give us a daily emblem of the circuit of our destiny, and had sent us daily to deliver it his messenger, Sleep the brother of Death. . . . Tired with the glare of the young Sun, we look to our old Mother night. . . . Whilst on the

---

36. From the *Vorrede* to the *Ideen zur Philosophie der Geschichte der Menschheit*, Suphan edition, vol. 1 (Hildesheim: Georg Olms, 1967), p. 11.

37. *Two Note Books of Thomas Carlyle*, ed. Charles Eliot Norton (New York: Grolier Club, 1898), p. 4.

38. Quoted in "Characteristics," *Essays* 3:38.

39. *Two Note Books*, pp. 33–36.

Earth she obscures the eyes of our body, she awakens the eyes of our soul to wide prospects of other worlds.[40]

Carlyle stops to comment that there is "*something* very sweet in it," and remembers Herder has written a Prize-essay about the origin of speech[41] and another about the decay of taste, from which Mme de Staël borrowed. Then he proceeds in his transcribing-translating:

> But as to the place and hour of thy future existence, fret not thyself O man; the Sun which illuminates thy day measures out for thee thy dwelling and thy earthly business, and obscures for thee meanwhile all the stars of Heaven. Soon as he goes down the world appears in its wider form: the sacred Night in which thou once layest shrouded up and wilt again lie shrouded up covers thy Earth with shades but opens for thee in its stead the shining books of Immortality in the sky.

(Herder is developing the Psalmist's great figure—the heavens *declare* the glory of God—into stars as shining *books* declaring immortality.)[42] Carlyle includes eight lines of Herder's verse (translated into his own eight verse-lines) that assert the changeless character of the stars and the evanescence of things here beneath in contrast. And then he continues in prose:

> Already hast thou in this Earth enjoyed much good. In it thou hast obtained that form of being, in which as a son of Heaven it is allowed thee to look around about thee and above. Seek then to leave it in contentment. . . . Thou hast no further claim upon it; it has no further claim on thee: crowned with the cap of freedom and girt with the girdle of Heaven, take up thy pilgrim staff with cheerfulness, and go on thy way.

The attitude toward this "allegory" turns up in Emerson when he writes of language in *Nature*: "Particular natural facts are symbols of particular spiritual facts." Carlyle is close to Emerson in this.

In 1826 Carlyle comes more to grips with Herder and writes, again in the Note Books, "What shall I say of Herder's *Ideen zur Philosophie der Geschichte der Menschheit*? An extraordinary Book, yet one which by no means wholly pleaseth me. If Herder were not known as a devout man and clerk, his book would be reckoned atheistical." The Calvinist here recognizes that as a scientist Herder rejects literal-

---

40. From Herder's *Nemesis*, Carlyle tells us.
41. *Abhandlung über den Ursprung der Sprache* (1770).
42. See his *Der Geist der hebräischen Poesie* (1783).

ist and miraculous Christianity. Carlyle is on the way to discovering that there is yet a kind of "religion" possible—reverence and devoutness. "Everything is the effect of circumstances and organisation: *Er war was er seyn konnte!* [He was what it was possible for him to be!]" It might have seemed to Carlyle that Herder approached determinism here, and yet Herder means to invite the development in ourselves of all the particularly human capacities—to discover what we can be, though we shall never reach the end, for the possibilities are infinite. "The breath of life is but a higher intensation of Light and Electricity! This is surely very dubious, to say no worse of it. Theories of this and kindred sorts deform his whole work here and there." Here are Herder's scientific interests and his holism, which no doubt became less dubious to Carlyle as he developed his own natural supernaturalism. He continues his comments on Herder's *Ideen*:

> Immortality not *shewn* us, but left us to be hoped for, and believed by Faith. Yet this world, as he thinks, sufficiently explainable without reference to another: *Humanität* the great object of Nature in all her arrangements of society; from the Troglodytes to the wits of Paris and Weimar. *How* true is this? At least this ought to be *our* object. On the whole Herder shews much of it himself. If any thing he has a leaning to the *East*. But indeed he loves all men and all things: his very descriptions of animals and inanimate agencies are animated, cordial, affectionate; much more so those of *men* in their varied *Thun und Treiben* [doing and dealing], tho' perhaps the former are not less poetical.

Carlyle is discovering a "religion" that need not offend the scientific mind, and he will realize in the infinite marvels of human capacity, of *Humanität*, a sufficient ideal. Carlyle appreciates the breadth of Herder's *Einfühlung* (empathy) and the humanism of the man himself, to whom nothing human—and nothing in the cosmos either—was alien. "Strange ideas about the Bible and Religion; passing strange we think them for a clergyman. Must see more of Herder: he is a new species in some degree."[43] The strange ideas were in fact a rejection of orthodox supernaturalism and a vigorous and radical understanding of the function of metaphor and symbol, which had been stimulated in Herder by his reading of Robert Lowth's lectures *De sacra poesi Hebraeorum* (1753). There follow in Carlyle's Note Book no less than three pages of books to read drawn from

43. *Two Note Books*, pp. 72–73.

Herder,[44] including works of the Orientalists, who like Herder "leaned to the *East*."

We see Carlyle again in these Note Books musing on *werden* and *seyn* (becoming and being) (132); on "Truth immer wird, nie ist"— even the Christian religion *grows* (158); on the Herderian relationship of Religion to Poetry (188, 215); we see him developing his alternative religion in its various parts, "the grand perennial Communion of Saints" (246) appearing to be our solidarity in *Humanität*; we see him acquiring a Herderian sense of the radical function of the figurative, its self-making, world-making power: "Prodigious influence of metaphors! Never saw into it till lately. A truly useful and philosophical work would be a good *Essay on Metaphors*" (142). *Sartor Resartus* is, in a way, that essay on metaphors, culminating in its "Symbols" chapter.[45]

But it is to Goethe that Carlyle owes the real resolution of his religious questions. Herder remained a clergyman, but Goethe felt himself constricted by mere Christianity (and felt a definite distaste for gruesome aspects of the New Testament); with Olympian grandeur he participated in World Religion, just as he envisioned World Literature. Herder taught the embracement of all varieties of human phenomena and Goethe practiced it. When Carlyle writes to Goethe, sketching out his projected (but never completed) history of German literature, he explains:

> Under you and Schiller, I should say, a Third Grand Period had evolved itself, as yet fairly developed in no other literature, but full of the richest prospects for all. Namely a period of new Spirituality and Belief, in the midst of old Doubt and Denial; as it were, a new revelation of Nature, and the Freedom and Infinitude of Man, wherein Reverence is again rendered compatible with Knowledge, and Art and Religion are one.[46]

The Goethean locus classicus for the comparative idea is trebly acknowledged by Carlyle. It is the account of the "three reverences" in chapters 10 and 11 of *Wilhelm Meisters Wanderjahre*, intimately known to Carlyle from his having translated it, quoted and acclaimed by him in his Goethe essay of 1828 for giving "in poetic and symbolic style a sketch of the nature, objects and present ground of Religious

44. *Two Note Books*, pp. 74–77.
45. As Charles Eliot Norton observes in his note on the passage, in *Two Note Books*, p. 142.
46. *Letters* 5:106 (23 May 1830).

belief,"[47] referred to in the Odin-Hero lecture. Years later—in 1866—in his Inaugural Lecture as Rector at the University of Edinburgh he paraphrases it at length and says, "it has dwelt in my mind as perhaps the most remarkable bit of writing which I have known to be executed in these late centuries."[48]

So venerated a text merits close consideration. *Wilhelm Meisters Wanderjahre* (or Travels, in Carlyle's translation) is Goethe's late addition to the early novel, the considered product of his *gebildet* serene old age. We can read it conveniently in Carlyle's own translation, thereby getting his own perspective on it. The drift of the chapters in question is as follows: Wilhelm comes to visit the educational establishment in which he has placed his son Felix; he observes that the youngest children have been trained in an attitude of reverence to the sky, older ones to the ground, and the oldest to each other. There is a theory behind this behavior, Wilhelm learns: naturally, man is born to *fear*, but a religion based on mere degrading fear is no religion. With the higher thing, *reverence* (*Erfurcht*), man can "in paying honour, keep his own honour; he is not disunited with himself." Reverence, however, must be learned. (Herder had indicated that since man is distinguished by his capacities for language, art, and religion, he must undergo, unlike the animals, "the long childhood" to acquire his tradition.) The reverence for the sky, for what is above, "looks joyfully towards Heaven," acknowledging God. The second reverence, for what is under us, is for Earth, for its bounties, and for both the joys and sorrows of the human condition. The third, more advanced, is the reverence for comrades, for the structures of society that enable man "to stand forth, frank and bold; not selfishly isolated; only in combination with his equals does he front the world." (In this conception of religion as essentially social Herder and Goethe anticipate Durkheim.) Reverence is the worth, "the business of all true Religions."

In a reprise, Goethe shifts the "three" somewhat. "The Religion which depends on reverence for what is above us, we denominate the Ethnic; it is the religion of the nations and the first happy deliverance from a degrading fear: all Heathen religions, as we call them, are of this sort, whatsoever names they may bear." We hear in this the Herderian note of the cultural comparative anthropologist: the Judeo-

---

47. "Goethe" (1828), *Essays* 1:234.
48. *Essays* 4:473.

Christian line may be seen as more *entwickelt*, developed, than others
and yet still one among others, all of which do reverence, in various
myths and polytheisms, to powers they cannot control, forces that are
"not we." The Second Religion, which this time is the social one (the
order has shifted), is "denominated the Philosophical; for the philosopher stations himself in the middle" and is wise insofar as he is
cognizant of all that is above and below. "Here, as he surveys with
clear sight his relation to his equals, and therefore to the whole human
race; his relation likewise to all other earthly circumstances and
arrangements necessary or accidental, he alone, in a cosmic sense,
lives in Truth." (For this Herderian school, Universal History—"the
whole human race"—is man's proper sacred study; Germans wrote
Allgemeiner Geschichten, universal histories, and Carlyle is to see in
history the Bible of the new religion.) It is the Third Religion—this
time of the earth—that we call Christian, for the Christian religion
best manifests this reverence although it is by no means exclusively
the property of Christianity. It consists in being "patient with the
Earth"—that is, we are to accept our earthly lot and also

> to recognise humility and poverty, mockery and despite, disgrace and
> wretchedness, suffering and death, to recognise these things as divine; nay,
> even on sin and crime to look not as hindrances, but to honour and love
> them as furtherances, of what is holy. Of this, indeed, we find some traces
> in all ages: but the trace is not the goal; and this being now attained, the
> human species cannot retrograde; and we may say that the Christian
> religion having once appeared cannot again vanish; having once assumed
> its divine shape, can be subject to no dissolution.

Here is a developmental, Herderian, concept of history and a highly
unorthodox doctrine related to it: Christianity is but a stage of human
history, back from which we cannot retrograde but forward from
which we are bound to progress in the direction of Carlyle's anticipated "new evangel."

Having surveyed these "reverences," Wilhelm inquires of his instructors: "To which of these religions do you especially adhere?" "To
all the three," they reply. "To all the three. For in their union they
produce what may properly be called the true religion. Out of those
Three Reverences springs the highest reverence, reverence for oneself,
and those again unfold themselves from this; so that man attains the
highest elevation of which he is capable." Here we recognize the
doctrine of *Bildung* and *Humanität*: that man, by being uniquely

endowed with these characteristic faculties—for language, for society, for religion, for art—has a kind of duty to develop all sides of himself harmoniously in all those capacities that distinguish his humanity. Out of this is to develop Matthew Arnold's ideal of culture as human salvation; and culture includes religion.[49]

To Wilhelm's questions, his instructors answer: "Our confession has already been adopted, though unconsciously, by a great part of the world. . . . For the first Article is Ethnic, and belongs to all nations; the second [of the earth], Christian, for those struggling with affliction and glorified in affliction; the third [the social], in fine, teaches an inspired Communion of Saints, that is, of men in the highest degree good and wise." Here, his "third" religion, in the Christian figure of Communion of Saints, is in fact the communion of solidarity in the humane tradition, Universal History of World Literature, Herderian *Humanität*. The "good and wise" who leave us this bequest are to develop into Carlyle's "Heroes." The "three-ness" can be variously represented, as the three great religions Lessing categorizes (Jewish, Christian, Moslem), or as here in this chapter: "Should not therefore the Three Divine Persons, under the similitudes [metaphors] and names of which these threefold doctrines and commands are promulgated, justly be considered as in the highest sense One?" Trinity now becomes a metaphor for Herderian holism, for the solidarity of *Humanität*, and for the Transcendental All.

Wilhelm then proceeds into a great gallery whose walls are covered with paintings of events from the "Sacred Books of Israelites." His leaders explain that "the spirit of it is to be sought for in the history of the world; its outward form, in the events of that history. Only in the return of similar destinies on whole nations, can it properly be apprehended." This is an invitation to the very study that the German school of biblical criticism was engaged in: Jewish history in the context of other histories, in the Herderian perspective of cycles ("the return of similar destinies on whole nations"). Alongside the pictures of Old Testament events are pictures from other cultures, "not so much synchronistic as symphronistic" (like-minded): beside "Abraham receiving a visit from his gods in the form of fair youths" is "Apollo among the herdsmen of Admetus. . . . From which we may learn, that the gods, when they appear to men, are commonly unrecognised of them." And from which the reader may learn the

---

49. See my *Arnold and God* (Berkeley: Univ. of California Press, 1983).

method of comparative folklore. Both Goethe and Carlyle would have been well aware of a "symphronistic" New Testament example of Christ on the road to Emmaus; the motif in question is what the folklorists call the "heavenly visitor." Wilhelm's leaders explain that Israelitish religion has the advantage over *other Heathen* [sic] religions in the excellence of its sacred books. And here Goethe speaks for his own often-recorded delight in the books of the Bible, and for Carlyle's too: "They are complete enough to satisfy; fragmentary enough to excite; barbarous enough to rouse; tender enough to appease!" We note that for Goethe as for Carlyle the values of the Bible are literary, not literalist.

In observing this gallery Wilhelm is said to have "the spirit of universal history before his mind"; he has the perspective, that is, if not of eternity, of the long humane tradition. He rejoices that his son Felix will learn all this by "visible representation, to seize and appropriate for his whole life those great, significant and exemplary events, as if they had actually been present, and transacted before him." And Wilhelm himself "came at length to regard the exhibition altogether with the eyes of the child, and in this point of view it perfectly contented him." For, we may comment, he knows as the German comparativists did that in the childhood of man, in primitive periods, man sees experience in pictures and stories—in *myth*. Grown men can continue to be "content" with these myths, understanding them as symbolic of truths otherwise difficult to grasp or ineffable.

Wilhelm inquires about the "life of the divine Man" and is led into another gallery representing the New Testament. "Here," says his guide, "you behold neither actions nor events, but Miracles and Similitudes. . . . By Miracles and Similitudes, a new world is opened up. Those make the common extraordinary, these the extraordinary common." And Wilhelm is afforded an explanation of the matter of miracles, a great stumbling block for *Aufklärer* and for Victorians in a crisis of faith:

> There is nothing more common and customary than eating and drinking; but it is extraordinary to transform a drink into another of more noble sort; to multiply a portion of food that it suffice a multitude. Nothing is more common than sickness and corporeal diseases; but to remove, to mitigate these by spiritual or spiritual-like means, is extraordinary; and even in this lies the wonder of Miracle, that the common and the extraordinary, the possible and the impossible, become one. With the

Similitude again, with the Parable, the converse is the case: here it is the sense, the view, the idea, that forms the high, the unattainable, the extraordinary. When this embodies itself in a common, customary, comprehensible figure, so that it meets us as if alive, present, actual; so that we can seize it, appreciate it, retain it, live with it as with our equal,—this is a second sort of miracle, and is justly placed beside the first sort, nay perhaps preferred to it.

This is Goethe's refusal to be reductive, granting a sort of heuristic validity to the miracle. It is classed with the similitude, as though to suggest it too is a kind of metaphor. But metaphor proper, or similitude, is the greater thing. Carlyle's choices of "similitude" for translating the word *Gleichnis*, likeness, here may well come from his familiarity with the great prophets so sympathetic to his mind and office, with Hosea, for instance: "I have multiplied visions, and used similitudes, by the ministry of the prophets" (Hosea 12:10). And metaphor, the way of the prophets and of the great poets, is "a second sort of miracle, . . . preferred to it. Here a living argument is pronounced, a doctrine which can cause no argument: it is not an opinion about what is right and wrong; it is Right and Wrong themselves, and indisputably." Symphronistically, Sir Philip Sidney had said: "The Poet never lieth, for he nothing affirmeth." Carlyle, great exploiter of metaphor, has one of the clearest appreciations of its function in art, in literature, and in religion—and he intimates its sufficiency.

Wilhelm notes that the representations in this New Testament gallery stop short of the Crucifixion and Resurrection; he is told that the student is made briefly aware of this area—of mystical experience—and knows "where more is to be had, should such a want spring up within him." But "the life of this divine Man" can be sufficient as pattern and example. The idea of Jesus as pattern gained a new currency in the nineteenth century, for it is a way of taking Christianity without any supernaturalism. The medieval meditational handbook by Thomas á Kempis, *The Imitation of Christ*, enjoyed considerable popularity as a religious exercise that would not offend the scientific mind.[50] Goethe had an extreme distaste for the Crucifixion, as perhaps Carlyle had too, and so veils it by what

---

50. Maggie Tulliver reads it. So does the Jewish actress Rachel, and so does Matthew Arnold. See *The Mill on the Floss*; Arnold's *Poems*, ed. M. Allott (London: Longmans, 1979), p. 524, and Arnold's *Collected Prose Works*, ed. R. H. Super, 11 vols. (Ann Arbor: Univ. of Michigan Press, 1960–1977), 3:133 et passim.

Carlyle is later to call a "sacred silence."[51] The whole episode ends with no ending but rather with the prospect of a return visit and further illumination; Carlyle says it gives him the notion of a *completed fragment*.[52] We might call it a deliberate atonality, and this in itself is a figure for Goethe's sense of *Bildung*, the self-development that is never complete—a *Werdende*, a becoming, not a being—because the capacities of man are infinite and because the capacities for the development of mankind are likewise infinite.

51. "The Hero as Divinity," *Heroes, Works* 5:11. See my discussion in chapter 6, "Odin."

52. *Essays* 1:233.

3. The Perspective of Universal History

Carlyle's theory of history has been richly studied; I want only to throw it here into a somewhat new perspective, that of comparative religion. German Historicism itself came out of an impulse that was in origin religious but by no means comparative-religious. The Herrnhuter brethren, or Moravians, were similar to Wesley and his Methodists, whom they influenced: both groups deplored the nonbelieving Enlightenment on the one hand and dry institutionalized orthodoxy on the other, and both insisted on felt experience and "the religion of the heart." In Germany, however, the new movement seemed to foster the intellect more than in England. In case after case, we see how the great exemplars of the new German learning came out of a pietist matrix; Goethe himself was exposed to it, as the "*Schöne Seele*" section of *Wilhelm Meister* shows. The universities of Britain were few and constricted by a dry orthodoxy, but in Germany they were many and highly developed, so that Carlyle himself sees a tremendous contrast: "Learned, indefatigible, deep-thinking Germany, [and the] unshackled, and even sequestered condition of the German Learned, which permits and induces them to fish in all manner of waters, with all manner of nets."[1] This is, in fact, academic freedom: no area, no method is barred. When sons of German pietist families, destined typically for the clergy (like Carlyle in Scotland), went to the universities, they took their pietist *Ernst* into the world of learning. If the Bible, in this land of Luther and Protestantism recently invigorated by the pietist movement, is to be the sole guide to faith, then it is the most urgent matter to ascertain the best text: out of this study comes a great wave of philological research into the languages of the Near East; out of this research comes linguistic evidence that various

---

1. *Sartor Resartus*, pp. 6, 8.

parts of the Old Testament were written in widely varying times of history and that Moses in fact could not have written all the Pentateuch, as pious tradition has it. Hence comes the need to study history, geography, and archaeology for their evidence as to biblical meanings and, with the growing sense of multiplicity and variety of cultures, to study cultural anthropology for the cultural conditioning of this supreme Document.

Since "to know one is to know none," as Goethe said of languages and as Max Müller said of religions, to know Judaism and Christianity we must study non-Jewish, non-Christian cultures, especially of the surrounding peoples. And so there flourished the great school of Orientalism. And then finally all science is urgently motivated to place the Bible and its events (the Crucifixion, say) in cosmic perspective—the largest historical perspective. The concept of Development (*Entwicklung*) was itself developed to accommodate Christianity to the cosmic perspective: we can grant that Christianity is better, or "higher," because it comes later.[2] Even developmental physiology is relevant. Goethe and Herder collected and contemplated animal bones, and Goethe made a discovery about the development of the jawbone of the ape into that of man. *Entwicklung* in fact anticipates Darwinian evolution. Even Christianity has developed and *will* develop, like all things in creation. The various impulses—philological, historical, biological, anthropological, aesthetic, and literary—were all mutually interactive and together made that great German period that is comparable only to Periclean Athens or Renaissance Europe. They are Titans of Letters, these great men—Lessing, Herder, Goethe, Schiller, the Schlegels, the Humboldts, Hegel, Schleiermacher, and the rest—great in their fields as their contemporary Beethoven is in music.

The core of Historicism has been defined as

> the recognition that all human ideas and ideals are subject to change, and this leads to the rejection of the stable, transcendent norms to which medieval Christianity had clung, and which in a secularized form the rationalist philosophers of the Enlightenment had maintained. Historicism is now identified with cultural relativism.[3]

Since to know the Bible and Christianity one must know other scriptures and religions and their cultures, scholars now practiced

2. The still later development of Islam made a difficulty here, generally slurred over.

3. Georg G. Iggers, "Historicism" in *Dictionary of the History of Ideas*, ed. Philip P. Wiener (New York: Charles Scribner's Sons, 1973), p. 457.

Allgemeine Geschichte, Universal History, to show the variations and the perspective of the whole. Herder's *Ideen* is the greatest, with its whole cosmic and biological sweep. In human history he includes even the Far East, China, and does in fact extend his *Einfühlung*—as he said it was the function of the historian to do—into an astonishing range of cultures. All this is impressively far ahead of British philistine parochialism: "Better fifty years of Europe than a cycle of Cathay," sings Tennyson in the sceptred isle. Johannes von Müller, who was Herder's friend and follower, did a *Universal History* in twenty-four volumes,[4] small accessible volumes (*Bändchen*) but very large in scope. Like Herder he gave emphasis to the history of religions and extended broad *Einfühlung* to all.[5] Goethe admired Müller, and Carlyle seems to have read him extensively. His *History* was translated into French and English, and Emerson said it was "much the best of all the universal histories."[6]

Carlyle's own base in fervent Scotch piety, his devotion to his pious parents, his original plan to study theology, and the gradual "unshackling" of his vigorous intellect in the libraries of Edinburgh give him his own particular driving impulse to investigate history. The Calvinistic brand of pietism, moreover, raises the issue of free will in a particularly pressing way. And so he reaches out to this Universal History of the Germans, with a religious motivation, and he borrows the perspective of Herder and Müller. In Müller's first extensive foray into *Religionsgeschichte* we find rhetoric that Carlyle seems to have borrowed:

> The human spirit, which measures the distance of the stars, which separates the presumed elements, which embraces the knowledge of the whole past, determines the opinions and the fates of millions and affects the far distant future, where does it come from? Where does it go to? Man has appropriated the lightning from heaven, extended earthly rule over the sea, computed the tracks of comets, penetrated the high regions of air; and who are we? Whence? Whither our goal? Our minds are dumb on these things. Formulas for [various] abstract systems, are better or worse

4. *Allgemeiner Geschichten*, 6 vols. (Stuttgart: Cottaschen Buchhandlung, 1831).
5. Meinecke, who doesn't think much of him, notes his work is "reminiscent of Herder's . . . historical outlook, with its basis in religion" (*Historism*, trans. J. E. Anderson [London: Routledge and Kegan Paul, 1972], p. 237).
6. Quoted by Thomas Grütter, *Johannes von Müllers Begegnung mit England* (Basel: Helbing and Lichtenhaln, 1967), p. 205. Lord Acton says he "is the first man to see history as a whole, . . . he is the man who achieved where Voltaire attempted" (p. 206).

thought, said, compared, and nothing seems more certain than uncertainty.[7]

Here is the Counter-Enlightenment insistence on our *lack* of knowledge and the mystery Carlyle espouses in his sense of man's destiny, "Who am I; what is this ME? . . . Whence? How? Whereto?"[8] out of Eternity, into Eternity. Right after this passage Müller speaks of *grossen Männer*, great men, whose achievements in literature extend even a millennium to give a fuller sense of life to mankind; his terms call to mind Herder's *Kette der Bildung*, the saving "chain of culture" that links us through the ages in *Humanität*, and one imagines Carlyle's idea of "Heroes" developing in this German context.

Carlyle is to become a "historian"—in *The French Revolution, Past and Present*, his *Cromwell* papers, and *Frederick the Great*. But in all his early work he is, I propose, the historicist historian already. History is our *Bible*, as he is to explain in *Sartor*: it is only in history that we get our understanding of religion, that is; and we need a prophet—or historian—to interpret it. Herder had said art, or literature, is the most precious, most significant achievement of a culture and *makes* the culture. The study of literature, then, is the study of history; and as Carlyle says, religion is "but a branch of literature."[9] All his significant early essays on writers are studies of "history," then, pursued with a religious urgency in the large cosmic perspective of Universal History. They tend to center on single great literary figures, for history is the biographies of great men. And it is great men, "heroes," who give meaning and continuity to human culture, unique in the animal kingdom for its continuity and progression. In the popular view, undue emphasis has been given to the political and military aspect of Carlyle's "heroes"; the basic concept of the hero is he who gives cultural continuity and so reinforces the solidarity of mankind. Napoleon's influence burned out with his life; Goethe's is infinite.[10]

In the early essays, then, mostly on German subjects, we may trace his developing comparativism. The essay on Jean Paul Richter (1827)

7. *Allgemeiner Geschichten*, part 2, bk. 9, p. 95. We find Carlyle in a letter of 26 April 1840 to Geraldine Jewsbury recommending Müller's history specifically because "he shadows out, with clearness and brevity, some of the best German ideas on the history of religion" (in a forthcoming volume of the *Letters*).

8. *Sartor*, p. 53.

9. See chapter 1 above, p. 6.

10. Essays 2:373. In this chapter references to the *Essays* will be in the text in parentheses: volume number and page.

(1:1–26) sketches the life and works with a humor and verve suitable to the extraordinary subject. Carlyle notes Richter's *Vorschule der Aesthetik* and explains this new term *aesthetics*, current now among the Germans. "Perhaps we also might adopt it; at least if any such *science* should ever arise among us" (1:10). For Carlyle, who already saw poetry and religion intertwined, such a science would be of first importance; as "criticism," he says it has been established in Germany by Winckelmann, Kant, Herder, and the Schlegels. One smiles to recognize in Carlyle's description of Richter's style how intimate this subject is, for it is Carlyle's own Sartorial style:

> Figures without limit; indeed the whole is one tissue of metaphors, and similes, and allusions to all the provinces Earth, Sea and· Air; interlaced with epigrammatic breaks, vehement bursts, or sardonic turns, interjec-tions, quips, puns, and even oaths! A perfect Indian jungle it seems; a boundless, unparalleled imbroglio. . . . Every work, be it fiction or serious treatise, is embaled in some fantastic wrappage, some mad narrative accounting for its appearance, and connecting it with the author, who generally becomes a person in the drama himself, before all is over. (1:12)

Carlyle broaches the impossible subject of humor, which is Rich-ter's "ruling quality," and lays it out for us, as mysterious as religion in its loving interchange with earth and man. "The last perfection of our faculties"—he quotes Schiller—"is that their activity, without ceasing to be sure and earnest, become *sport*" (1:16). And of his favorite humorists he refers to Shakespeare, Swift, Sterne (Sterne is "our best," Carlyle's special favorite, and so influential in Germany), Cervantes; in Germany, Lessing has a "genial" share of humor and Goethe has now a "rich true vein"; but there is none that in depth, copiousness, and intensity of humor can be compared with Richter's. He "lives, moves, and has his being in it" (1:18). (Laughter came easily to the Carlyles, a ground of being for them as for Richter.) Rejoicing in his author's variety and eccentricity, he celebrates his particularity in a very Counter-Enlightenment way, quoting Lessing: "Every man has his own style, like his own nose" (1:19); he uses the German idiom of *Bildung*: "The great law of culture is: Let each become all that he was created capable of being. . . . There is no uniform of excellence, either in physical or spiritual Nature: all *genuine* things are what they ought to be" (1:19). *Er war was er seyn konnte.*

He works up to Richter's "philosophy." Though Richter may seem the rankest of infidels, he reveals "a noble system of Morality, and the firmest conviction of Religion" (1:22). And what sort of Religion is it? He quotes: "Are all your Mosques, Episcopal Churches, Pagodas, Chapels of Ease, Tabernacles, and Pantheons, anything else but the Ethnic Forecourt of the Invisible Temple and its Holy of Holies?" (1:22). Comparative with a vengeance! He says Richter is religious "in the highest sense of the word . . . independently of all dogmas." And now we recognize that Carlyle is using Goethe's mode:

> A reverence, not a self-interested fear, but a whole reverence for the spirit of all goodness, forms the crown and glory of his culture. The fiery elements of his nature have been purified under holy influences, and chastened by a principle of mercy and humility into peace and well-doing. An intense and continual faith in man's immortality and native grandeur accompanies him. (1:22)

This is certainly a generalized religion that can subsist in varieties of clothes—mosques, pagodas, whatever; "the spirit of all goodness" seems to be an effort to name the common ground of differing ideas of God. The "immortality" can be understood only with the new German ideas of the immateriality of Space and Time; the "native grandeur" is Weimar humanism. Richter is a writer "for men that love truth, and will not accept a lie. A frank, fearless, honest, yet truly spiritual faith is of all things the rarest in our time" (1:23). The "fearless" man is one who is not afraid to deny the unbelievable supernatural elements in religion.[11] Richter will last, Carlyle says, and he cites three English writers on religion: Hooker, Jeremy Taylor, Sir Thomas Browne; their writings too will endure "when their way of thought has long ceased to be ours, and the most valued of their merely intellectual opinions have passed away, as ours too must do, with the circumstances and events in which they took their shape" (1:25). Dogma is evanescent; literature endures. The "merely intellectual" is mere clothes for enduring *Humanität*.

In 1827 Carlyle published in the *Edinburgh Review* the "State of German Literature," taking as his starting point Franz Horn's volumes on the subject. He weighs and describes Horn's lively style and notes his faults. Horn advocates the cause of religion, but "his zeal outruns his prudence and insight" (1:27); he declares that poets to be

11. René Wellek asserts that Carlyle was right in his high evaluation of Richter and recognizes that Richter's religious thought was the most important to Carlyle, his blending of philosophy and poetry into religion ("Carlyle and German Romanticism" [1929], in *Confrontations* [Princeton: Princeton Univ. Press, 1965], pp. 34–81, 66–71).

poets must be Christian. This leads only to scoffing; we are bound to ask "when Homer described the Thirty-nine Articles; or Whether Sadi and Hafiz were really of the Bishop of Peterborough's opinion?" (1:27) But Carlyle leaves Horn and goes on to do his own history and description.[12] Carlyle acclaims Lessing as "the noblest of sceptics . . . of a higher mood than had yet been heard" (1:48). He cites among other works Lessing's *Nathan der Weise* and pays tribute to its inspiration, Moses Mendelssohn, as a type of Socrates; he pays tribute also to Hamann. He acclaims the new German criticism, no longer concerned with surface minutiae but "proposing to itself a higher aim" (1:51); even the astounding achievements of such as Shakespeare (whose works are "truer than reality itself") are addressed "by rigourous scientific inquiry" (1:52). He acclaims the "aesthetic" theories of Kant, Herder, Schiller, Goethe, Richter, Tieck, the two Schlegels. Carlyle's emphasis on the word *Criticism* indubitably suggests its most famous brand, the Higher Criticism of the Bible, and implies that it too proceeds by "rigourous scientific inquiry." The mere existence of such a science is, he says, a "European tendency" (1:53), answering to widespread intellectual needs. The Germans, moreover, extend the field of literature: "Ferdusi and the primeval Mythologists of Hindustan live in brotherly union with the troubadours and ancient Storytellers of the west" (1:54). It goes without saying here that in extending literature to include the Persian epic and the Sanskrit classics, we will also have to extend our understanding of the religions they embody. And in what must be granted to Carlyle as a perfectly sound "History of Ideas," he epitomizes the radical historicist attitude:

> The Germans study foreign nations in a spirit which deserves to be oftener imitated. It is their honest endeavour to understand each, with its own peculiarities, in its own special manner of existing; not that they may praise it, or censure it, or attempt to alter it, but simply that they may see this manner of existing as the nation itself sees it, and so participate in whatever worth or beauty it has brought into being. (1:55)

---

12. Werner Leopold takes this essay as a turning point (*Wendepunkt*) in Carlyle's career (*Die Religiöse Wurzel von Carlyles literarischen Wirksamkeit, dargestellt an seinen Aufsatz "The State of German Literature" (1827)*, Morsbachs Studien zur englischen Philologie 62 [Halle: Max Niemeyer, 1922], p. 113). Leopold finds Carlyle's analysis both original and sound. See also Leopold's Appendix to C. F. Harrold's *Carlyle and German Thought: 1819–1834* (1934; reprint, London: Anchor Books, 1963), p. 238.

The Germans, accordingly, have the best and most numerous translations.

Art is respected in this society because it is "the highest in man" (1:48). "To inquire after its *utility*, would be like inquiring after the *utility* of a God, or . . . the *utility* of virtue and Religion" (1:56). He quotes Schiller's *Aesthetic Education of Man*: "Man has lost his dignity, but Art has saved it, and preserved it for him" (1:57). He quotes Fichte's *Nature of the Literary Man*: writers are "a perpetual priesthood . . . standing forth generation after generation, as the dispensers and living types of God's everlasting wisdom . . . in such particular form as their own particular times require it in" (1:58). He acclaims the "Göttingen school" (1:50), Herder, Schiller, Goethe, and an age of German writers comparable in greatness to our own Elizabethans. Goethe especially reveals to us the Spirit of the Age; and Carlyle quotes Goethe's poem: "all Nature's thousand changes / But one changeless God proclaim" (1:67). He takes up the charge of mysticism so often made against the Germans, noting that the label *mystical* applied by the English could be better taken to mean *not understood* (1:70). While there are indeed German mystics, such as Novalis and Böhme, it is patently absurd to label as mystics great men like Kant and Fichte—Kant, "the vigilant clear-sighted," trained (as was Carlyle) in mathematics, and Fichte, "cold, colossal, adamantine spirit . . . fit to have been the teacher of the Stoa" (1:77)! Carlyle here anatomizes Kant's differentiation of *Verstand/Vernunft* (understanding/reason) in his own way; although he was later to discount the terms, the distinction was important in his thinking at the time. He consistently preaches the limits of logic or understanding, "the merely intellectual" as he calls it in the Richter essay. In that essay as here he affirms that there is another power—*Vernunft*—whose domain is where logic and argument cannot reach, "that holier region, where Poetry and Virtue and Divinity abide" (1:83). Finally he concludes (in the passage quoted in part in chapter 1):

> To the charge of Irreligion . . . the Germans will plead not guilty. On the contrary, they will not scruple to assert that their literature is, in a positive sense religious; nay, perhaps to maintain, that if ever neighbouring nations are to recover that pure and high spirit of devotion, the loss of which . . . can be hidden from no observant mind, it must be by travelling . . . in the same direction in which the Germans have already begun to travel. . . . Religion, Poetry, is not dead; it will never die. (1:84–85)

The essay on Zacharias Werner, quoted above for its important Herderian-Müllerian statement that "every Creed, every form of worship, is a form merely; the mortal and everchanging *body*, in which the immortal and unchanging *spirit* of Religion is" (1:143) belongs to this period—to 1828. "Goethe's Helena," a short essay about an interlude in *Faust*, has an important passage that illustrates Carlyle's concept of myth. The story of Faust, he says, can be considered part of "the Christian mythus, in the same sense as the story of Prometheus, of Titan, and the like, are Pagan ones" (1:154). Now, he says, it is hard to imagine how the story "must have harrowed up the souls of a rude and earnest people, in an age when its dialect was not yet obsolete"—that is to say, in the primitive age when the myth is believed literally.

> The day of Magic is gone by; Witchcraft has been put a stop to by act of parliament. But the mysterious relations which it emblemed still continue; the Soul of Man still fights with the dark influences of Ignorance, Misery and Sin; still lacerates itself, like a captive bird, against the iron limits which Necessity has drawn round it; still follows False Shows, seeking peace and good on paths where no peace or good is to be found. In this sense, Faust may still be considered as true. (1:155)

This is historicist cyclism: when a society no longer believes in its anthropomorphic gods literally, the husks (or *clothes*) of things may be discarded to reveal the vital truth they had "emblemed" or made apprehensible to a people who needed images and stories. What Carlyle does here is *demythologize*, and he does it very deftly. The subject is now the marvelous old story of Faust and Mephistopheles; the method, it is suggested, can apply to the images and stories of the Bible. We can interpolate: "In this sense the Bible—may still be considered as true."

In 1828 Carlyle writes a long essay on Goethe, quoting at length and commenting on his own favorite text, the tenth and eleventh chapters of the *Wanderjahre*, the "Three Reverences." The essay recounts the career of Goethe, beginning with the Byronic *Werther* that leads to suicide. That Goethe wrote it indicates in itself his superseding of that phase—as *Dichtung und Wahrheit* recounts. And in *Wilhelm Meister* the problem has been solved: "Anarchy has now become Peace . . . ; he has conquered his unbelief; the Ideal has been built on the Actual" (1:224). He presents Wilhelm's extravagant discourse on the poet, from the *Lehrjahre*:

> Fate has exalted the Poet . . . as if he were a god . . . the Poet is a teacher, a
> prophet, a friend of gods and men. . . . [Poets] found a home in every
> habitation of the world. . . . The hero listened to their songs, and the
> Conqueror of the Earth did reverence to a Poet; for he felt that, without
> poets, his own wild and vast existence would pass away like a whirlwind,
> and be forgotten forever. . . . Nay, . . . who but the Poet was it that first
> formed Gods for us; that exalted us to them, and brought them down to
> us? (1:226–28)

We may note that this charming apotheosis is in fact Goethe's playful
appropriation of Herder's expressionism: the primitive poet *makes* in
his metaphors our gods and our world—in the Old Testament, in
classical myth, in Northern myth.

Carlyle pays tribute to Goethe's long career—fifty years from
Werther to the *Wanderjahre*, the "emblematic intellect," the univer-
sality, the freedom (like Shakespeare's) from mannerism—and speaks
in the clearest terms of Goethe's saving power for Carlyle himself:

> Goethe has not only suffered and mourned in bitter agony under the
> spiritual perplexities of his time; but he has also mastered these, he is above
> them, and has shown others how to rise above them. . . . He was once an
> Unbeliever, and now he is a Believer; and he believes, moreover, not by
> denying his unbelief, but by following it out; not by stopping short, still
> less turning back, in his inquiries, but resolutely prosecuting them. (1:210)

How this has come about is the vital concern of our time: "How has
the belief of a Saint been united in this high and true mind with the
clearness of a Sceptic; the devout spirit of a Fénelon made to blend in
soft harmony with the gaiety, the sarcasm, the shrewdness of Voltaire?" (1:210). In Goethe,

> there is embodied the Wisdom which is proper to this time; the beautiful,
> the religious Wisdom, which may still, with something of its old im-
> pressiveness, speak to the whole soul; still, in these hard, unbelieving
> Utilitarian days, reveal to us glimpses of the Unseen but not unreal World,
> that so the Actual and the Ideal may again meet together, and clear
> Knowledge be again wedded to Religion, in the life and business of men.
> (1:208)

We may note Carlyle's sense of process, of development, and of his
own career as a recapitulation of Goethe's: through the necessary
atheism to the serene Goethean godlike vantage point, as *Sartor*
recounts.

The Burns essay also belongs to 1828 and is full of the most interesting, loving, acute comment on his countryman's poetry. But— he quotes Milton: "He who would write heroic poems must make his whole life a heroic poem"—Burns failed. What did he lack that Milton had, that Cervantes had? One, a "true religious principle of morals" and, two, "a high heroic idea of Religion, of Patriotism, of heavenly Wisdom, in one or the other form"; a "Deity . . . , the Invisible Goodness, which alone is man's reasonable service" (1:312– 13). The term "Invisible Goodness" certainly seems to hark back to deistic generality and the well-known absentee Watchmaker; but what is new in Carlyle is the sense of immanence of this Invisible Goodness and the sense that Invisible Goodness is honestly served in any one of the various changing forms. Burns

> has no Religion; in the shallow age where his days were cast, Religion was not discriminated from the New and Old Light *forms* of Religion; and was, with these, becoming obsolete in the minds of men. His heart, indeed, is alive with a trembling adoration, but there is no temple in his understanding. He lives in darkness and in the shadow of doubt. His religion, at best, is an anxious wish; like that of Rabelais, "a great Perhaps." (1:313)

"Old and New Light" refers to the wrangling sects of Scottish religion, which are mere *clothes*; the wrangling discredits all religion. Carlyle does not mention the marvelous "Holy Willie's Prayer," but that would illustrate the point. He does some belated vocational counseling: Burns should have stayed a peasant-poet and rejected the excise post and high society. "Byron and Burns were sent forth as missionaries to their generation, to teach it a higher Doctrine, a purer Truth" (1:316), but both failed us. "It seems to us there is a stern moral taught in this piece of history,—*twice* told as in our own time" (1:316). It is as though Carlyle will allow no poet to be secular. His warm, discriminating appreciation of Burns—and of Byron too, for that matter—may seem at odds with his moralism; the point is that he sees them as illustrative of his historicism. Where they failed, Goethe triumphs.

The last essay dated 1828 is a long study of the scholar as hero, Christian Gottlob Heyne, who gave us the standard text of Homer. He is in a German tradition that Arnold is to remark especially: the great scholars, men such as Wolf and Wilhelm von Humboldt, took an active hand in shaping common education.[13] Heyne, Carlyle notes, from his post in the University of Göttingen remodeled the Gymnasia and furthered the administration and interaction of the universities. And Carlyle pictures the University with the same imagery he uses in *Sartor Resartus*: "An establishment for universal science . . . , a watchtower where a man might see all the kingdoms of the world" (1:320–21)—which sounds like Universal History. Heyne's own scholarship made a new epoch in classical studies; he is

> the first who with any decisiveness attempted to translate fairly beyond the letter of the Classics; to read in the writings of the Ancients, not their language alone, or even their detached opinions and records, but their spirit and character, their way of life and thought; how the World and Nature painted themselves to the mind in those old ages, how in one word, the Greeks and the Romans were men, even as we are. (1:350–51)

Thus Heyne, "by his inquiries into antiquity . . . , its politics and its mythology," has carried the torch of Philosophy. What Winckelmann is to ancient Art, Heyne is to ancient Literature. Once more Carlyle implies more than he says. German scholarship, as is well known, established rigorous methods for the classics and then applied those methods with equal rigor to the Bible. In fact, the study of Homer and the Bible offers striking parallels: multiple authorship, for instance, was propounded for Homer just as for the Pentateuch, and figurative interpretations often supplanted the literal. So when Carlyle characterizes Heyne as going "beyond the letter," he implies biblical scholarship—which also extended to *politics* and *mythology*, to the writers as *men*, and to the special and variable shifting cultures that produced Scripture.

In 1829 Carlyle produced "German Playwrights," a dutiful overview and a warning that plays are but the "froth and scum" of German literature; he then addressed religious questions again in three connecting essays, "Voltaire," "Novalis," and "Signs of the Times." After an informed and sympathetic survey of Voltaire, he comes to the point: Voltaire is prominent chiefly "as a vehement opponent of the Christian Faith" (1:455) and understood nothing of it but the superficies. For him, it all turned on "plenary Inspiration of the Scripture" (1:457); but the wiser minds of the age now agree

13. See Arnold's *Schools and Universities on the Continent*, vol. 4 of *Collected Prose Works*, ed. R. H. Super (Ann Arbor: Univ. of Michigan Press, 1960–1977), p. 223, et passim.

that Christianity has been recognized as divine on far different grounds. Its meanings, as Voltaire could not imagine, "every new age will develop to itself in a new manner and with new degrees of light; for the whole truth may be called infinite" (1:458). (Pure Herderism!) We cannot, he says in Goethe's terms, *retrograde* from it: "In every pure soul, in every Poet and Wise Man, it finds a new Missionary, a new Martyr, till the great volume of Universal History is finally closed" (1:459). But we must be tolerant of Voltaire as of all men and their cultures; his "chief merits belong to Nature and himself; his chief faults are of his time and country" (1:460). His task was "Denial . . . destroying and overturning" (1:459). And so Carlyle sees Voltaire as part of the cyclical process that in destroying the old assists in the birth of the new. Superstition passes away, extirpated by the necessary Atheism, thereby revealing Religion ever more clearly.[14]

In the Voltaire essay, Carlyle quotes Novalis contra Voltaire: the mechanistic Universe is rejected, and we see rather

> beauteous and many coloured . . . Poesy, like a leafy India, when contrasted with the cold, dead Spitzbergen of that Closet Logic. . . . [We] recognize and again preach forth the sacredness of Nature, the infinitude of Art, the independence of Knowledge, the worth of the Practical, and the all-presence of the Spirit of History. (1:467)

Here is a very broad kind of "sacredness" or religion. And the Novalis essay quotes Novalis extensively. Carlyle's stance is a little like the Editor's with Teufelsdröckh: I do not altogether endorse or even understand this but will set it forth for consideration. But the essay is rich in religious musings. In its denial of the existence of matter, he says, German idealism was anticipated by Berkeley, and before that by the ancient Pyrrho, the modern Hume, and, "as Sir W. Jones informs us, . . . the theologians of Hindostan."[15] Carlyle underwrites the nonexistence of Time and Space, for thereby (we may observe) is removed a stumbling block to conceiving of Deity as omnipresent and eternal, and "Atheism melts into nothingness" (2:26). Our mysterious Novalis in his "strange Oriental delineations" (2:32) reminds him of Herder and then of Pascal. Like Pascal (and like

14. The essay "Diderot" (1833), which is delightfully informed and acute on the subject's career and personality and works, is on the matter of religion perfectly parallel to the Voltaire essay. By exhausting the line of atheism, both Diderot and Voltaire make the issues more clear.

15. William Jones, who learned Sanskrit and was the great precursor of the Germans in comparative philology.

Carlyle) he moves from mathematics to religion. And we see, in a passage quoted from Tieck on Novalis, the prototype of the religion of *Sartor*: "For him it had become the most natural disposition to regard the commonest and nearest as a wonder, and the strange, the supernatural as something common; men's every-day life lay round him like a wondrous fable" (2:53). In conclusion Carlyle considers the prediction that "the belief in God will be like that in nursery Spectres," or, "as Jean Paul has it, 'Of the World will be made a World-Machine, of the AEther a Gas, of God a Force, and of the Second World—a Coffin'" (2:54). But Carlyle rather thinks "such a day will *not* come"; Enlightenment reductionism is on the way out. Let there be free scope for Mysticism such as that of Novalis. "A fair field and no favour, and the right *will prosper!*" (2:55).

This phase of Carlyle's culminates in "Signs of the Times," where he gathers together into his prophetic vein the strands of what we call history of ideas and what he called in *Sartor* "Things in general." "O ye hypocrites, ye can discern the face of the sky; but can ye not discern the signs of the times?" (Matthew 16:3). Carlyle values the function of metaphor in our lives, and even in our religions;[16] and he details the contemporary dryness of utilitarian mechanistic attitudes and the intellectual self-sufficiency that boasts of "the daylight of truth"— which turns out to be the mere flicker of "closet-logic" (a phrase from the Novalis essay).

> Now all this is grounded on little more than a metaphor. We figure Society as a "Machine," and that mind is opposed to mind as body to body; whereby two, or at most ten, little minds must be stronger than one great mind. Notable absurdity! . . . *One* man that has a higher Wisdom, a hitherto unknown spiritual Truth in him, is stronger, not than ten men that have it not, or than ten thousand, but than *all* men that have it not; and stands among them with quite ethereal, angelic power, as with a sword out of Heaven's own armory, sky-tempered, which no buckler, and no tower of brass, will finally withstand. (2:75)

So much for the utilitarian quantifying mind! We recognize here the germ of the Heroes-doctrine: single great individuals change the world: Jesus, Mahomet, Luther. Meantime, "Wonder" (from Novalis again) is dying out. Religion, which is properly "a thousand-voiced psalm from the heart of Man to his invisible Father, the fountain of all

---

16. George Lakoff and Mark Johnson, *Metaphors We Live By* (Chicago: Univ. of Chicago Press, 1980).

Goodness, Beauty, Truth" (2:76), is no longer what it should be.[17] Literature, too, then, is in a bad way. But there is always change, and an ultimately progressive development. "We have a faith in the imperishable dignity of man; in the high vocation to which, throughout this earthly history, he has been appointed. . . . Our spiritual maladies are but of Opinion; we are but fettered by chains of our own forging, and which ourselves also can rend asunder" (2:80). (Compare Blake's "mind-forged manacles.") There are signs of a brighter era, when mechanism will not be our taskmaster but our servant. Now there is "a boundless, grinding collision of the New with the Old. The French Revolution, as is now visible enough, was not the parent of this mighty movement, but its offspring" (2:82). Mere political freedom has been its ostensible object, but there is a "higher, heavenly freedom" in prospect.

Carlyle wrote for *Fraser's Magazine* two pieces, "On History" and "On History Again," in 1830 and 1833 respectively, that remind us of the context of all his other studies. Clio, he tells us, as eldest daughter of Memory and chief of the Muses, indicates history is "the first product of man's spiritual nature" (2:83), whether the man is Celt, Copt, Red man or white; man looks before and after and "would fain unite himself in clear, conscious relation, with the whole Future and the whole Past" (2:83). This most demanding of human functions is yet the most difficult: its material is "the ever-living ever-working Chaos of Being" (2:88), and while all action is multidimensional, all narrative is linear. So while history is said to be "Philosophy teaching by experience," the philosophy—we would say the principles or the hermeneutics—must precede the teaching. "History is a real Prophetic Manuscript, and can be fully interpreted by no man" (2:90); we may infer principles but must not fancy that they "exhaust the matter." We see here the modern concept that even history is a making of "fictions," that all histories and theories must be *provisional.* There are strong Herderian elements: "The inward condition of Life [culture, extrasomatic knowledge] is the same in no two ages" (2:86); in the "chains and chainlets" (Herder's *Kette der Bildung*), those connections of things that Carlyle is to develop into "Organic Filaments,"[18] we see "mysterious vestiges of Him whose path is in the great deep of Time" (2:89) (Herder's *Spur* of the Maker). Like Herder's too is the

17. Joseph Campbell's study of mythology is called *The Hero with the Thousand Faces.*
18. *Sartor*, pp. 244–53.

sense of infinitude: that is why human accomplishments must be always provisional, never complete or absolute; and like Herder's is the sense of Literature and Religion as overlapping entities, forming together the most important achievements of cultures. "Art also and Literature are intimately blended with Religion. . . . He who should write a proper History of Poetry, would depict for us the successive Revelations which man had obtained of the Spirit of Nature" (2:94). There are many aspects of history: while political history has been the main line, it now gives way to others, ecclesiastical history, for instance. As performed so far, ecclesiastical history concerns too much "the outward mechanism, the mere hulls [Herder's *Hülle*]"; and Carlyle suggests what would be, rather, a universal comparative history of religion. The artists in History are those who keep the eye for the Whole, "the Idea of the Whole, and habitually know that only in the Whole is the Partial to be truly discerned" (2:90)—in Universal History.

"On History Again," from 1833, is more *rusé* and sportive, more in the vein of Diogenes Teufelsdröckh. Here Carlyle's Müller is put alongside the great seventeenth-century moralist Bossuet and his *Histoire universelle*, but in an intellectual leap Carlyle presents even the limits of universal history in a hierarchy of infinitude. "All Universal History is but a sort of Parish History which the . . . Clerk of this Parish, member of our Alehouse Club . . . puts together" (3:168). "The River of Existence is so wild-flowing, so wasteful" (3:169), and by the miraculous faculty of speech, of writing, we make and read history, "the Letter of Instruction . . . the Message, verbal or written which all Mankind delivers to every man" (3:167). Universal History is a "magic web" (3:175), ever changing, as Tacitus is revised and renewed by Montesquieu, Livy by Niebuhr, and—nota bene—Moses by Eichhorn, who was a notable Higher Critic of the Bible. It is "the true Epic Poem, and universal Divine Scripture" (3:176).

As might be expected, the religious issues are clearest of all in Carlyle's essays on Goethe.[19] Musing on the portrait of Goethe, he sees "the clearest, most universal man of his time [; in] that head the whole world lies mirrored . . . and revealed authentically to be still holy, still divine . . . , a mad universe of scepticism, discord, despera-

19. "Goethe's Helena" (1828); "Goethe" (1828); "Goethe's Portrait" (1832); "Death of Goethe" (1832); and "Goethe's Works" (1832).

tion, *transmuted* into a wise universe of belief, and melody, and reverence" (2:371–72). He died a hero's death: he had just "called for paper for the purpose of writing and expressed his delight at the arrival of spring" (2:374)—two kinds of worship, we might add: *laborare* which is *orare*, and a joyful "wonder" in nature.

Changes are gradual and not immediately clear, but now the age of Hume as "pontiff" is ending. There have been *two* great men in our time: Napoleon destroying and Goethe remaking chaos into a creation. Napoleon's influence blew itself out in twenty-five years, but Goethe's death has no effect on his influence. "Nay, upon this earth of ours there have been men whose Impulse has not completed its development till after fifteen-hundred years, and might perhaps be seen individually subsistent after two thousand" (2:378). Out of this guarded statement emerge certain unequivocal points: Jesus was a man like other men; Christianity *developed* or changed; it was completed, as it were, with Luther; and Jesus may well be a personality to be reckoned with centuries hence. "Such a *man* [my italics] became, by Heaven's pre-appointment, in very deed the Redeemer of the time" (2:379). He even suggests that Jesus' ordeal in his time was parallel to Goethe's: Jesus "was filled full with its scepticism, bitterness, hollowness and thousandfold contradictions, till his heart was like to break; but he subdued all this, rose victorious over this, and manifoldly by word and act showed others that come after, how to do the like" (2:379).

Goethe's death, like all deaths "the palpable revelation of the mystery of wonder and depth and fear" (2:386), invites the view sub specie aeternitatis; the fifth act casts a new meaning over the other four. For an interpretation Carlyle brings in none other than Diogenes Teufelsdröckh! This could be a wistful puff for *Sartor*, soon to come out in *Fraser's Magazine*; it is also, as it is supremely in *Sartor*, a means of self-protection, a guardedness, so that Carlyle may not be held accountable for the views to follow. And we Carlyleans can be warned therefore that what follows will be unorthodox. Teufelsdröckh insists that "reverently man loves man, and daily by action evidences his belief in the divineness of man" (2:388). Out of this comes his religion, "Hero-Worship"; "it is the only creed which never and nowhere grows or can grow obsolete" (2:389). Atheism is impossible; man must worship something and sees the Infinite in the finite. Man is the clearest symbol of Divinity, and (quoting Novalis) man is "what the Divine Man is called in Scripture, a 'Revelation in the

Flesh'" (2:390). Carlyle keeps the perspective universal, with comparative-religion references to Chaldeans and Zoroaster, to the Hindoo devotee and the Egyptian leek-worshipper.

Goethe was a hero for his own complicated and confusing time because of his prodigious many-sidedness, with his informed cultivation of History, of Science, of Art; his functions as poet, courtier, politician, man of business; and—as we know—his adherence to "all the three religions" or all possible religions, a model, we might say, of *Bildung* and *Humanität*. His "works" are the subject of the longest of these essays. Since, Carlyle says, "the greatest work of every man is the Life he has led" (2:402), he recounts Goethe's life at some length, tracing roughly a parallel to the life of Jesus and then more precisely a parallel to the life of Diogenes Teufelsdröckh as we know it in *Sartor Resartus*. And so this essay is a variant of *Sartor*, close to it in time, less poetic and more discursive. There is use of the metaphor of *clothes* and, still more interesting, there is comment on metaphor itself. "Goethe is full of *figurativeness*," not in an "ornamentary" literary way but even in the way he uses the common language. "Goethe's figurativeness lies at the very centre of his being; manifests itself as the constructing of the inward elements of a thought, as the *vital* embodiment of it" (2:437–38). Like Shakespeare, he "constructively comprehends" a thing,

> can take it asunder, and put it together again; the thing melts, as it were, into light under his eye, and anew *creates* itself before him. That is to say, he is a thinker in the highest of all senses: he is a Poet . . . . The world lies encircled with WONDER; the Natural in reality the Supernatural, for to the seer's eyes both become one. (2:437)

In Goethe's final period, "Reverence becomes triumphant" in *Meister's Wanderjahre*, as we know, and also in the late poetry, the *West-östlicher Diwan*. Carlyle pretends to quote a critic, but we know he is quoting himself and guarding himself in order to make a daring statement about this late poetry, "which, it has been said, for pregnancy and genial significance, except in the Hebrew Scriptures, you will nowhere match" (2:431). Finally, this "universal man" leaves us a treasure "of faith become hope and vision":

> The question, Can man still live in devoutness, yet without blindness or contraction; in unconquerable steadfastness for the right, yet without

tumultuous exasperation against the wrong; as an antique worthy, yet with the expansion and increased endowment of a modern? is no longer a question, but has become a certainty, and ocularly visible fact. (2:440)

This Goethe essay looks forward to *Heroes and Hero-Worship* and the "divine" in man.

4. Carlyle's Early Histories

All Carlyle's works, early and late, are imbued with a sense of Universal History, the Herderian cosmic perspective of infinite Space and Time. *Sub specie aeternitatis* takes on fresh meaning as a motto for his oeuvre. The periodical essays we have reviewed are so conceived, as are all his other early works. One project was a history of German literature that Carlyle knew himself uniquely qualified to do; he was possessed with the idea of transmitting Goethean salvation. The German essays surveyed above would have been part of it, with two others, "The Nibelungenlied" and "German Literature of the Fourteenth and Fifteenth Centuries," both of 1831.[1] He spent the years 1828 to 1832 vainly seeking support and a publisher for such a history. He was anticipated in the market by the industrious William Taylor of Norwich and his three-volume *Historic Survey of German Poetry, Interspersed with Various Translations.*

In 1831 Carlyle found himself reviewing this work for the *Edinburgh Review.*[2] In this galling situation he does not stint his own vastly superior knowledge or gloss over Taylor's shortcomings. Taylor gives no history; he calls the Middle Ages *dark* (Carlyle knew better); he is full of mistakes; he is out of date; he has no feelings for Religion or Poetry (coupled as usual): he is, in sum, an utter *Philister*, says Carlyle, making nice use of this German student slang for the enemy of culture. Washing his hands of this "all-too-sordid" subject of Taylor, Carlyle concludes: the mere existence of Taylor's work is a sign of the new era. "Instead of isolated, mutually repulsive National Literatures, a World Literature" becomes possible (a Goethean idea), "a tendency to a universal European Commonweal"; "the true Poet . . . is the inspired Thinker . . . , an Orpheus. . . . Literature is fast

1. *Essays* 2:216–73 and 274–332.
2. *Essays* 2:333–70.

becoming all in all to us; our Church, our Senate, our whole Social Constitution" (2:369).

It is much to be regretted that Carlyle received no support for his projected history of German literature. His considered treatment of Lessing, Hamann, Jacobi, and Herder would have been rich resources to have at hand. However, we do in fact have some of his manuscript, a fair-sized work edited with copious notes and published by Hill Shine in 1951.[3] It consists of an opening chapter on literary histories; a second chapter on the German people; a third on "Traditionary Lore" and the German language, with some demonstrations of the Gothic proto-German and some translations of *Märchen*; and some chapters on the medieval era. When in the opening chapter Carlyle says it is the words "Let there be light" that *make* things visible, he is presenting an expressionist theory of literature and indicating that the Bible is one part of literature among others. He quotes Goethe again: "Who but the Poet was it that first formed gods for us; that exalted us to them, and brought them down to us!" Literature *is* Traditions, Mythologies (and, we understand, Religion), "the earliest and noblest product of man's spiritual nature . . . , the element in which mind lives and moves"; it "unites the Past with the Present; and the scattered Present into one whole . . . ; of separate Men it makes Nations and Mankind." Closely echoing Herder, he says a national literature "is not only the noblest achievement of the nation, but also the most characteristic; the truest emblem of the national spirit and manner of existence." He presents Goethe's vision of World Literature:

> Surely the time will come when nations instead of regarding themselves as natural enemies, will find that they are natural friends . . . , all brothers and fellow soldiers engaged . . . in one mighty ever enduring warfare against Necessity and Evil. . . . Literature is now not only our Grand Arsenal and Storehouse, wherein all that Time has done for us is to be preserved and turned to use; but it is becoming also, what is infinitely more, our grand Metropolitan Temple, where, if anywhere, all men are to meet and worship.

In this chapter on what might be called "theory of literature" he makes an apology for theory:

3. *Carlyle's Unfinished History of German Literature*, ed. Hill Shine (Lexington: Univ. of Kentucky Press, 1951). All quotations in the following paragraph are from pages 3 to 10.

> That tendency that we have to theorize on all things, to "account" for all
> things, is but our natural love of order, put in action; and blameless,
> praiseworthy, so it overstep not the limits. Nothing can be more natural
> than for a man to build himself some small theoretical Observatory,
> whence he may look around the world a little; only let him not try to reach
> the Heavens with it, otherwise it proves a Tower of Babel, and ends in
> confusion of tongues.

By demythologizing the Tower of Babel here, Carlyle makes the figure
communicate the idea of the limits of rationality. We must consider
our theoretical hypotheses to be provisional, or temporary heuristic *fictions*, as we call them now; they are not to be put forward
as dogma, for no science will ever give us mastery over "Literature,
Poetry, the Sphere-music of man's soul." "Philosophy overshoots
itself; in stretching our logical faculty to impossible lengths, we
pervert and neglect the province that really lies under its dominion."
The literary historian must limit himself, as a "witness to report and
intelligibly represent the things visible, as they successively or simultaneously emerge. . . . The primary causes and grand moving agencies
[should be considered as] a mighty sea . . . whose interior secrets, in
their bottomless depth, defy all sounding." Both theory and history
must respect their boundaries and respect the unknown, the unknowable, the mystery to which wonder and reverence are proper.

All Carlyle's work on the history of German literature contributes
in some way to the masterwork of *Sartor Resartus*. At the end of
chapter 1, after introducing the remarkable and mysterious volume
of Professor Teufelsdröckh, *Die Kleider, ihr Werden und Wirken*
(Clothes, their origin and influence), the Editor concludes, "Möchte es
auch im Brittischen Boden gedeihen!" (May it thrive also on British
soil!).[4] And what he offers in *Sartor is* the whole complex of German
historicist thought, in brilliant and sportive images that make it
count. It *did* thrive on British soil and changed the world for English-
speaking peoples. George Eliot's verdict is well known: if all Carlyle's
books were to be burned,

> it would be only like cutting down an oak after its acorns have sown a
> forest. For there is hardly a superior or active mind of this generation that
> has not been modified by Carlyle's writings; there has hardly been an

4. *Sartor*, p. 9.

English book written for the last ten or twelve years that would not have been different if Carlyle had not lived.[5]

After *Sartor Resartus*, Carlyle wrote a great chapter of Universal History, a book of his "Bible," in his *French Revolution* (1837). This is the working out of German historicist principles in practice, the vision of cycles, of Goethean alternating periods of belief and unbelief. The wonder is that so didactic a history is yet so respectable in its research and so compelling that it imposes itself on the reader's imagination. As David Daiches has said,

> Carlyle's vision of a great retributive force at the heart of things finally breaking out to manifest its stern justice in human history and then rounding on its own ministers when they in turn showed themselves incapable of the heroism and morality which the historical moment demanded—this vision . . . is the emanation of an incandescent historico-moral imagination.[6]

As his fame grew after the success of the *French Revolution*, Carlyle was persuaded (perhaps not quite as reluctantly as he claims in his letters) to speak from the public lecture platform. In accounts of his lecturing years we can detect Carlyle's growing sense of satisfaction: his Scots accent, his earnestness, humor, and lively style were good theater. The lectures of the first series, on German literature, were never published, but we may safely infer the drift of them from the essays on the subject; of the second series, given in 1838 on the History of Literature, we do have an interesting record. The third series, on the revolutions of modern Europe, was an extension of his *French Revolution*; and the fourth, where he came into his own as a performer, is our main subject, *Heroes and Hero-Worship*, which he revised and made into a book. Before turning to *Heroes* I want to consider the record of his lectures on the History of Literature. Knowing Carlyle's vision of Religion-Literature as a single complex, we might well surmise there is interest here for the comparative-religion question.

5. *Thomas Carlyle: The Critical Heritage*, ed. Jules Paul Seigel (London: Routledge and Kegan Paul, 1971), pp. 409–10, from an unsigned review in the *Leader*, 27 October 1855.

6. "Carlyle and the Victorian Dilemma," in *More Literary Essays* (Chicago: Univ. of Chicago Press, 1968), pp. 130–31. This was the Thomas Green Lecture to the Carlyle Society in 1963.

We have the lectures transcribed by a certain T. C. Anstey, who must have been very good at shorthand, for the text is very full and characteristic of Carlyle's style.[7] Carlyle builds a "theoretical Observatory" of Herderian periodicity and looks around him, or back rather, through the ages over the range of known civilizations. Much as he deplores "self-consciousness" elsewhere,[8] he shows himself beautifully self-conscious in the post-Kantian way, aware of the provisionality of his Observatory: "There is a very great difficulty in reducing this generation of thought"—*Geistesgeschichte*, history of ideas—"to a perfect theory,"

> as indeed there is with everything else, except, perhaps, the stars only, and even they are not reduced to theory; not perfectly, at least, for, although the solar system is quite established as such, it seems doubtful whether it does not in its turn revolve around other solar systems, and so any theory is, in fact, only imperfect. (2)[9]

This statement of Gödelianism, astonishingly prescient, recurs throughout his works; the insight alone earns him a secure place in the history of ideas. What we can legitimately do, he continues, is hypothesize: "We shall see this great stream of thought, bearing with it its strange phenomenon of literary production, divide itself into regular periods"(2). He anticipates our modern discovery that even when we think we are being most objective, we seize on and depend on certain root metaphors.[10] "Our Knowledge of physics, our whole circle of scientific acquirements, depends on what *figure* [my emphasis] each man will give it and shape to himself in his own heart!"(64)

And so he posits the acknowledgedly "imperfect" theory but the best or most adequate conceivable in his time, the theory of cycles and perpetual *Entwicklung*, the infinite *Werdende* (becoming) that distinguishes and unites mankind and describes ultimately a kind of spiral movement toward—God, the good—whatever (which Arnold later calls "Perfection"). Carlyle envisions the following cycles: the Greeks, from Homer and the heroic to the self-consciousness of Euripides and Socrates; the Romans, from Magna Graecia to the sack of Rome; the

---

7. *Lectures on the History of Literature* (New York: Scribner, 1892).

8. In "Characteristics," *Essays* 3:1–43.

9. In this chapter the numbers in parentheses are page numbers of the *Lectures on the History of Literature.*

10. See George Lakoff and Mark Johnson, *Metaphors We Live By* (Chicago: Univ. of Chicago Press, 1980).

Middle Ages, culminating in Dante; Protestantism, from Luther to the French Revolution; and *now*, a new beginning with the new heroic to be discerned in German literature. Carlyle's cyclical phases are not precise or neat; at times they interplay with Goethe's systole-diastole movement of alternating periods of belief and unbelief. At any rate, for Carlyle the unbelieving self-conscious stage culminates in dissolution generally cataclysmic and bloody; the French Revolution is the type of it.

Carlyle seems to have reviewed Johannes von Müller's *Universal History* for these lectures; he refers to him five times.[11] Müller's handy volumes would have given him a convenient chronological framework. Above all, Müller perpetuates the Herderian sense of the overruling weight of religion in cultural history. In his essay on Werner Carlyle referred to Müller's principle that "all systems of faith" are *Vorstellungsarten* (modes of representation) of the unchanging human essence of religion;[12] it becomes a key principle here. Moreover, we see Carlyle moving toward the opening declaration of *Heroes*: "A man's religion is the chief fact with regard to him." In these lectures religion seems to be the "chief fact" of history and of literature too. On Greek polytheism, he rejects Hume and Gibbon: "It is really, in my opinion, a blasphemy against human nature to attribute the whole of the system to quackery and falsehood"(12). Carlyle detects his idea of God in the Greek's recognition of a destiny (*moira*) "a great dumb black power"(14) overarching all the vagaries of their gods and men. For a rationalization of polytheism, he favors Euhemerism (11), the theory (named for Euhemerus of Sicily, c. 315 B.C.) that the gods were originally kings and heroes, later apotheosized. We shall see how he develops this in *Heroes*.

As he traces the Greek cycle, he elaborates on Homer as heroic and the *Iliad* as based in "a series of what I shall call ballad delineations" (16); the idea is Herder's idea of "folklore." Herder parallels Homeric ballad sources with folk writers of Old Testament poetry and of Northern balladry. As though elaborating on this comparative folklore, Carlyle says his own recent rereading of the Robin Hood material and the Italian *commedia dell'arte* has persuaded him they are the same kind of thing. He cites with approval Wolf's multiple authorship

---

11. *Allgemeiner Geschichten*, 6 vols. (Stuttgart: Cottaschen Buchhandlung, 1831), pp. 17, 20, 41, 108, 126.
12. *Essays* 1:143–44; and see above, chapter 1, p. 6.

theory of the *Iliad* (which ever implies the multiple human authorship of the Pentateuch). Aeschylus seems to join Homer in the heroic class, with some notable sentences of literary criticism: with Aeschylus, "you fancy that you hear the old dumb rocks speaking to you of all . . . they had been thinking of since the world began, in their wild, savage utterances" (32). Sophocles is more cultivated and chastened; with Euripides we are on the verge of disease, of an age of speculation and skepticism. Socrates completes the cycle: he "shows a lingering kind of awe and attachment for the old religion of his country, and often we cannot make out whether he believed it or not" (35). It is pretty clear here that Carlyle has considerable *Einfühlung* with Socrates and sees their situations as parallel parts of their cycles. Altogether, he says, Socrates "must have had a painful intellectual life" (35).

He covers the Roman cycle with comparisons as though of a metacycle: the Greeks were the *children* of antiquity, the Romans the *men*; the Greek religion was sportive compared to the devout and patriotic religion of the Romans; the Greek idea was *harmony*, the Roman idea *method*; and with the Romans the Empire was greater than their literature. "Their greatest work was written on the face of the planet in which we live" (49). Carlyle fails in his religious permissiveness in the case of Carthage: he is glad the Romans destroyed Carthage, for "their rites were perfectly horrid; their religion was of that sort so often denounced in the Bible" (49).[13] We glimpse the Jews, obstinately "clinging to the same belief, probable or improbable, or even impossible" (47). Virgil is less than Homer because Homer is greatly unself-conscious.[14] "In short, from the Christian religion down to the poorest genuine song there has been no consciousness in the minds of the first authors of anything of excellence" (51)—the statement is interesting for its quiet implication that Christianity is a *literary* creation. Tacitus closes the Roman cycle: standing "like a Colossus at the edge of a dark night," he noted the "hateful superstition" of the shabby Christian sect but noted also (very like Carlyle) "a kind of worth in the Germans" (56–57).

13. See "Child Sacrifice at Carthage," *Biblical Archaelogy Review* 10, no. 1 (January 1984): 30–51. Carlyle did not advance as far as twentieth-century ecumenicism, satirized in a Beatles movie as an Anglican garden party that includes polite dialogue with a convocation of politic cannibals.

14. This German cyclicism helps account for the Victorians' discounting of Latin writers in favor of the Greek, so impressive in Matthew Arnold.

The future lay with Christianity and the Germans. The next cycle, the Middle Ages, is no longer to be called *dark*, says Carlyle. We must note that the belief part of the cycle—in the Church of Rome— is pretty big this time: from the Fall of Rome to Luther. Carlyle feels he can make some points about medieval people: their devout beliefs, for instance, were utterly independent of dogma. (When Matthew Arnold some years later devalues dogma in favor of literature he is following the Carlylean line.) To appreciate medieval Christianity is not altogether to dismiss paganism, which had "much good" in it. In paganism one had belief in one's *self*; and the pagans "recognised in themselves . . . the existence of a Supreme Arrangement" (64)—this peculiar locution appears to demythologize both Zeus and Jehovah into their common ground in man's psyche. Stoicism and Cynicism, then, are much to be admired, but Christianity nevertheless represents an advance. "It is not our part to touch on sacred things, but"—this disclaimer *is* disingenuous on Carlyle's part, when his subject is almost steadily religious—

> but we should altogether fail to discover the meaning of this Historical Period if we did not lay deeply to heart the meaning of Christianity. In another point of view [not of sacred things?] we may regard it as the revelation of eternity existing in the middle of time to man. He stands here between the conflux of two elements, the Past and the Future; the thing that we are at this moment speaking or doing comes to us from the beginning of days. The word I am this moment speaking comes to me from Cadmus or Thebes . . . and it will go on to an endless future! . . . This truth, whatever may be the opinions we hold on Christian doctrines, or whether we hold on them a sacred silence or not, we must recognize in Christianity. (67)

From Christianity—as Goethe had said—we can never retrograde. (The peculiar expression "sacred silence" will recur in *Heroes*.) The point seems to be that Christianity envisages a linear development of history, or time-plot, from the Garden of Eden to Jesus to the Apocalypse. But it sounds less like Christianity than like Herderian cultural history, with the *Kette der Bildung*, the chain of culture, and the philological studies that traced the family of languages, and the implied parallel of families of religions: "One can fancy with what mute astonishment the invading barbarians must have paused when their wild barbarous minds were at first saluted with the tidings of that great Eternity lying round the world, this earth now become an intelligible thing to them" (68). And this conversion distinguishes "modern Europe from all the world besides." With some Germanic obscurity, Carlyle proceeds to claim that the Germans (and he includes all the northern peoples, of course) had a distinct aptness for Christianity.

Carlyle continues his medieval history with more attention to religion than to literature. He is "far from vindicating" the Crusades, he says, but their value is that in them Europe proved its belief (78)! He gives a sentence or two to the troubadours and trouvères and somewhat more to the recently discovered *Nibelungenlied*, the "finest poem" of the period. The lecture on Dante reaches toward a Hero-theory: we revere Italy for Raphael, Michelangelo, Columbus, Galileo; "the great thing which any nation can do is to produce great men" (86). Dante's poem will outlast Roman Catholicism (just as Homer outlasted paganism, I suppose): the doctrine of Purgatory, for instance, is unbelievable now. And yet—Carlyle demythologizes—it *means* that men "must believe in the inexorable justice of God, and that penitence is the great thing" (99). In connection with Spain, Carlyle takes the opportunity to speak of Moors and to assert that Mahomet was no impostor; the Mahomet of *Heroes* had been thought of long and well ahead of time. Meanwhile, he gives a sympathetic account of Cervantes and of *Don Quixote*, its humor and its burlesque of chivalry. He notes its popularity—of all books it is the most widely read except the Bible—and as though to explain that, he adds, "It is valuable . . . as a sort of sketch of the perpetual struggle of the human soul. We have the hard facts of this world's existence, and the ideal scheme struggling with these" (117–18). It is the archetypal struggle, we might say—and therefore religious in Carlyle's broad sense.

In dealing with the Reformation, Carlyle again gives more history of religion than of literature and enunciates principles, the familiar ones that lie behind *Sartor*. Progression is the law of man, and no one creed can be perpetual or complete. A creed will expand until men discover things inconsistent within it; then there is uneasiness of mind and ultimately spoken protest. "When the mind begins to be dubious it will rush with double rapidity toward destruction" (130)—one senses Carlyle's own experiences of those youthful days of destructive doubt in Edinburgh. There are always "inferior men" with vested interests in the status quo—and it was against these men that Martin Luther stood forth. We can understand Luther to be a hero of literature, but Carlyle only touches on his great translation of the Bible, concentrating on his heroic public career. Essentially Luther asserts "the right of consulting one's own conscience, which every new founder of a civilization must now take along with him, which has entered largely into all the activity men have had since!" (137) Erasmus gets a little space, but beside Luther he is a mere "littérateur"; Ulrich von Hutten gets four pages, and he is "not in literature at all." Such is this history of—religion.

When he comes to England, Carlyle sees a cycle similar to that of Rome and an empire that outdoes the Roman, triumphant over the globe and over Nature as well through its technology. King Alfred is acclaimed a great ruler and, for his translations, a man great in literature as well. Carlyle comes, *con amore*, to Shakespeare—earlier, greater, more "heroic" than Milton. He is characterized in terms of the theme of religion. "One does not find what religion he was of; an universal believer, impressed with many things which may be called religions; having reverence for everything that bore the mark of Deity, but of no particular sect, not particularly Protestant more than Catholic. But Milton was altogether sectarian" (165). Shakespeare as "universal believer" sounds like the Goethean ideal, with a subscription to, at the very least, "all of the three." John Knox gets five pages; he is a hero for his courage and for his sincerity, for having "civilized" Scotland and for having brought "into the meanest minds, into every bit of Scotland, the greatest thoughts that ever were in the mind of man" (164).

Our man Anstey had to miss the lecture on France, but the editor of 1892 feels we may gather the substance of it from Carlyle's essays on Voltaire and Diderot. And so we come to England in the eighteenth century, a time of disbelief less "baneful" in England than in France because the English teutonic nature is slower and deeper and because England as a Protestant free country is better regulated than France! But it was a time of disputation, contrariety, and argument, when logic was felt to be supreme. Logic, however, can be supreme in one area only: mathematics. In all other areas logic is insufficient, simply because our terms are not precise or stable as number is. The pretense of logic ends in "niaiserie" or delusion. So it was a time of inferior literature but great achievements, such as Arkwright's and Watts's inventions and Whitfield's Methodism (why not Wesley's?). Dryden was a great poet in the worst of times, Addison a mere lay preacher, and Steele only his second. Swift got into the Church with no vocation and "was a kind of cultivated heathen, no Christianity in him" (177). Sterne failed in his clerical duties, but "we cannot help feeling his immense love for things around him," and "much is forgiven him"— as well it might be, for his great influence on the German writers and on Carlyle himself. Johnson, the great conservative, "contrived to be devout" in this unlikely time and is a hero in that; and we love Boswell for loving him. Hume is the opposite pole from conservative Johnson, being the great puller-down and yet useful in defining skepticism. Gibbon is futile, with his view of the world as "a huge imbroglio of quackery" (184). These logicians had pretended to account for everything till, in Jean Paul's words, "Heaven became a gas, God a force, the second world a grave" (191). Carlyle puts forward his diagnosis tentatively, warning again that "his history of European culture" is not intended as a final account. The overvaluation of logic resulted in *Wertherism*, the doctrine of defeat. Logic leads to suicide. In England, Byron represents this phase (as Seneca did in Rome's similar cycle).

What comes next, then; what comes now? "I think I shall show you that there is a new thing" (205)—this is his introduction to the last lecture, "Modern German Literature." He invokes the Phoenix-rebirth figure and gives us yet another version of *Sartor Resartus*. He recapitulates the cycles he has outlined: Greece from Homer to Socrates; Roman paganism and empire to the Fall of Rome; the Middle Ages, culminating in Dante; and Protestantism, culminating in the French Revolution—"the burning up of scepticism." The saving new literature of Germany gives us no *one* answer or theory but rather the "thrice blessed phenomenon of men unmutilated in all that constitutes man, able to believe" (210). I think this is best referred once more to Herder's *Humanität* and the ideal of *Bildung*—that man is unique in creation for the infiniteness of his capacity, uniquely capable of language, of religion, of social institutions, of art, of morality. And in Goethe Carlyle finds the broad humanism that looks beyond personal happiness. Hume and Diderot are merely destructive; Kant (Carlyle revises his earlier ambiguities) seems simply pointless as he reverses the nay-sayers and asserts that *all* is spirit (214). But Goethe is near to Shakespeare in "clearness, tolerance, and humane depth." Goethe turns his youthful sufferings into belief and action. *Wilhelm Meister* shows his early conviction that "ideal art" is the highest good; but in the continuation, the *Wanderjahre*, he, being near seventy, writes luminous chapters on religions, "all the three." Carlyle reveres these chapters because they restore Christianity to the apex of things, but a Christianity that does not offend the intellect. The wise man can be the devout man—cannot fail to be one.

Carlyle speaks here too of Goethe's lovely late poetry, the *West-östlicher Diwan*: "It is in form a Mahometan-Persian series of delineations, but its whole spirit is Christian. . . . The whole gathers itself up in the end into what Goethe thinks on matters at large" (217). The very last poem of the *Diwan*, we may note, is a "Gute Nacht!" where the poet is charmingly apotheosized into a *Paradies*, "mit Heroen aller Zeiten" (with the heroes of all times). We see in this poem Goethe's all-embracing *Humanität*, taking to itself *all* the human tradition, and we see in it also a foreshadow of Carlyle's *Heroes*.

This "History of Literature" looks like a History of Religion, and the reason is that salvation is in Literature—which includes scriptures. In the lecture on the English Renaissance Carlyle declares himself free of Coleridgean categories: "I know that there have been distinctions drawn between intellect, imagination, fancy and so on, and doubtless there are conveniences in such a division, but . . . the mind is *one*" (156). Poet and thinker, god, prophet, priest—all heroes—are one and the same human stuff. Religion and Literature are undifferentiated in the infinite, ever-changing heritage of the human tradition.

5. "Little did my poor mother know"

Carlyle was particularly well placed to appreciate Herder's notion of the heroic value of folk poetry since he grew up in an area that has some of the grandest folk poetry, the Scottish border ballads. The ballads were enjoying new respect through the work of Sir Walter Scott and—more to Carlyle's taste—their actual recycling by Burns. They were established as part of the voice-and-piano repertoire of musical households in England,[1] and they were esteemed in the Carlyles' house in Chelsea. One of them in particular was loved by Carlyle, the magnificent "Mary Hamilton" or "The Queen's Maries." It is as haunting as ever now in the version I learned orally from a member of the clan McLeod who learned it orally from her great-grandmother—and in the version sung some years ago by Joan Baez. It is the story of the queen's waiting woman seduced by the king and later hanged for the murder of a child.

> Word is to the Kitchen gone
>   And word is to the hall
> That Mary Hamilton's borne a babe
>   To the highest Stuart of all.
> . . . .
> Yestreen the Queen had four Maries;
>   The nicht she'll hae but three.
> There was Mary Beaton and Mary Seaton
>   And Mary Carmichael and me.

---

1. See Patrick Piggott, *The Innocent Diversion: A Study of Music in the Life and Writings of Jane Austen* (London: Douglas Cleverdon, 1979). Scottish songs were typically part of social life for the Austen family and their friends.

O little did my poor mother know
  The night she cradled me
That I should die so far from home
  Or hang on a gallows-tree.

There are two kinds of ultimate horror for a Scottish Calvinist family: one is the seduction of a daughter, classically portrayed in Scott's *Heart of Midlothian*; the other is an offspring's loss of faith. And the classic case of the latter is Carlyle's. What makes it so is the extreme intensity of the family's fundamentalist faith, combined with the signal love and devotion reigning there and Carlyle's own high principles and searching intellect, what he called his love of truth. Religion of the pietist, literalist, and strictest sort was truly the "chief fact" with his parents; they were unwaveringly convinced, not without a certain fundamentalist logic, that the loss of faith of a beloved child was far worse than any worldly calamity, for it would result in the perpetual flames of hell. The young Carlyle's powers of intellect were recognized and respected; financial sacrifices were made; and it was expected that he would become a clergyman. And then we see him away from home, at the University of Edinburgh, reading Gibbon and Hume and the French rationalists, working himself by degrees into terrible straits between an intellect he acknowledged to be God-given and the old impossible supernaturalist certainties of home, with its circle of beloved faces.

In the Chelsea Carlyle house there has been deposited a pane of glass from a window in Carlyle's Moray Street student lodging in Edinburgh, on which is incised with a diamond point:

Little did my mother think
  That day she cradled me
What land I was to travel in
  Or what death I should die.

In his Note Book for 31 December 1823 he writes: "The year is closing; this time eight and twenty years I was a child of three weeks old lying sleeping in my mother's bosom." And he quotes the same four lines of the ballad, this time with the Scots *mither* for *mother*. He continues:

Another hour and 1823 is with the years beyond the flood. What have I done to mark the course of it? Suffered the pangs of Tophet almost daily. . . . Another year or two and it will do. . . . "Then why don't you kill yourself

Sir? Is there not arsenic? Is there not ratsbane of various kinds, and hemp and steel?" Most true, Sathanas, all these things *are*: but . . . you observe Sir I have still a glimmering of hope; and while my friends (my *friends*, my Mother, Father, brothers and sisters) live, the duty of *not* breaking their hearts would still remain to be performed when hope had utterly fled.[2]

Even at this time he was engaged in reading the Germans—a glimmering of hope seemed to come from that direction. He saw instances of reverence for the things his parents revered, in minds that were moving freely among everything intellectual, "fishing in all kinds of waters, with all kinds of nets," and he dedicated himself to finding the secret of this reverence. Much later, the ballad, still associated with his mother, continues to haunt him. In the Anstey record of lectures on the history of literature, Carlyle is touched by Ulysses' encounter with the elusive shade of his mother Anticlea: "In all nations we read or hear of such feelings as that; we go for them into the heart of human nature. The same sentiment, for instance, we meet with in those beautiful lines of the 'Queen's Marys.'"[3]

Still later, in 1842, a painting of his mother that Carlyle had commissioned arrived from Scotland. Carlyle was delighted with the likeness and set about arranging to install it over the living room mantelpiece of the Chelsea house. Jane objected violently and won her point. "I could never feel alone with that picture over me! I almost *screamed* at the notion."[4] It is a powerful painting, "my good old Mother exactly as she looks; with her air of embarrassed *blateness* [shyness], yet of energy, intelligence and true affection";[5] indeed it is horrendously powerful, with a searching intensity of surveillance. We can imagine such an image in Carlyle's mind ever since his youth. It would be enough to strike dumb a lesser man. We might speculate that many promising young Victorian atheists went mute and in-glorious to the grave for fear of paining a fundamentalist parent. John Seeley published his *Ecce Homo* (1865), a reverent but non-

2. *Two Note Books of Thomas Carlyle*, ed. Charles Eliot Norton (New York: Grolier Club, 1898), pp. 55–56. The note on the ballad, p. 55, reads: "To this, Carlyle in 1866 appended the words 'Extract by Burns—*first* came to me thro' T. Murray.' T. Murray was his first intellectual friend, met on the way to Edinburgh in 1810." See *Letters* 1:4.

3. *Lectures on the History of Literature* (New York: Scribner, 1892), p. 24.

4. From Fred Kaplan, *Thomas Carlyle: A Biography* (Ithaca: Cornell Univ. Press, 1983), p. 314.

5. Kaplan, p. 314.

Margaret Carlyle. Painting by Maxwell of Dumfries, c. 1842. Courtesy of the Carlyle House, The National Trust for Historic Interest or Natural Beauty, London.

supernaturalist view of Jesus, anonymously, to save the feelings of his fundamentalist father.

Carlyle found another way. He discovered a mode, a "dialect" that solved the problem. In the German school he found a basic emphasis on *metaphor*: for Hamann, God as "Poet at the beginning of days" is the Metaphor-Maker; we are encompassed by symbols everywhere in all nature, and "the true Shekinah is man."[6] For Herder, the "folk" expressed their most sacred experience and sense of nature in metaphors—anthropomorphs, myths. Language itself is from the start pervasively metaphorical. The scholars of the Schleiermacher school of Higher Criticism of the Bible appreciated all biblical miracles and other impossibilities as metaphors of spiritual meanings. This complex of the all-importance of figures becomes progressively more important to Carlyle. "Prodigious influence of metaphors!" he exclaims in his Note Book about 1828. "Never saw into it till lately. A truly useful and philosophical work would be a good *Essay on Metaphors*. Some day I will write one!"[7] As Charles Eliot Norton observed, that essay was to be *Sartor Resartus*.[8]

In *Wotton Reinfred*, the abortive first novel of 1826 not published till after Carlyle's death, where we see him awkwardly working out some of his problems of expression, the theme of belief is paramount. Our hero Wotton is contrasted with his friend Bernard: "The former never believed, the latter never doubted." With Bernard, "that he wished a thing to be true was ever with him a strong persuasion of its truth. He sympathized with Wotton's scepticism; often he seemed, with a deep sigh, to admit that his objections were unanswerable, yet himself continued to believe. . . . It seemed to Wotton, he would practise cunning subterfuges, and . . . play jesuitic tricks with his own convictions."[9] As for Wotton-Carlyle, "his love of truth . . . had ruined him; yet he would not relinquish the search to whatever abysses it might lead . . . ; he wandered in endless labyrinths of doubt, or in the void darkness of denial. With other men his conversation was stinted and irksome, for he had to shroud his heart from them in deepest mystery."[10] Carlyle also had to shroud his heart from his

6. *Sartor*, p. 66.

7. *Two Note Books*, p. 142.

8. In his footnote to the passage, *Two Note Books*, p. 142.

9. *Wotton Reinfred*, in *Last Words of Thomas Carlyle* (London: Longmans, 1892), p. 28.

10. *Wotton Reinfred*, p. 31. Further references in the text below are to page numbers.

mother. (We might call this particular anguish Wotton's Complaint.)
In his later *Life of Sterling* (1851), Carlyle has mastered this subject
and writes more freely of a case parallel to Wotton's: the tragedy of
Sterling's life in his particular epoch is that "his love of truth ruined
him." Carlyle talks of that high-principled love of truth in men such as
Sterling:

> Speedy end to Superstition,—a gentle one if you can contrive it, but an
> end. What can it profit any mortal to adopt locutions and imaginations
> which do *not* correspond to fact; which no sane mortal can deliberately
> adopt in his soul as true; which the most orthodox of mortals can only, and
> this after infinite essentially *impious* effort to put-out the eyes of his
> mind, persuade himself to "believe that he believes"? Away with it; in the
> name of God, come out of it, all true men![11]

And now we turn back to 1819; he is writing to his mother from
Edinburgh:

> I am rather afraid that I have not been quite regular in reading that best of
> books which you recommended to me. However last night I was reading
> upon my favorite Job; and I hope to do better in time to come. I entreat you
> to believe that I am sincerely desirous of being a good man; and tho' we
> may differ in some few unimportant particulars: yet I firmly trust that the
> same power who created us with imperfect faculties, will pardon the errors
> of every one (and none are without them) who seeks truth and righteous-
> ness, with a simple heart.[12]

This reveals the set of his mind. The "few unimportant particulars"
are dogma that might seem quite important to *her*; but to him the
essential is the determination to be "good." He implies graciously that
either his *or* her intellect may be defective, and he cannot but believe
what his God-given faculties lead him to believe. He will seek truth
with a simple heart: that is, he will not "play jesuitic tricks with his
own convictions"; he will not "put-out the eyes of his mind." He can
truthfully tell his mother he reads Job and that it is his favorite because
in fact Job's heroism consists in just that: adamant refusal to play
tricks with his own convictions or to put out the eyes of his mind, even
in the teeth of the whole familial and religious establishment.
Of course the Book of Job is his favorite. It shapes his idiom:

11. *Life of Sterling*, *Works* 11:51; referred to by volume and page numbers in the
text.
12. *Letters* 1:174.

phrases like "the land of the living" and "the wicked cease from troubling" are more frequent in his writings than in ordinary literate English. It may also shape his vision of self. He sees himself repeatedly as a type of Job the Sufferer, more or less patient. The book requires no dogmatic Christian commitment; it is nearly impossible to read literally, even for the fundamentalist. It is one of the greatest and longest-lived of literary monuments, extending our brotherhood back into Babylonian days. It affords a supreme example of a myth, or fiction, obviously untrue, that has, notwithstanding its fictionality, the greatest meaning for the human situation. It is the text, the scripture of Carlyle's religion of Wonder.

In *Wotton Reinfred* Carlyle pictures Coleridge in the guise of a character called Dalbrook, a sort of Kantian blowhard, presented ambiguously. Sometimes he is "a man of wonderful gifts . . . on the whole a splendid nature, yet strangely out of union with itself. . . . His very speech displays imbecility of will" (80). And at other times he sounds like Carlyle himself.

> Much of this which you call Kantism seems but the more scientific expression of what all true poets and thinkers, nay, all good men, have felt more or less distinctly, and acted on the faith of, in all ages. . . . What is all religion but a worship of the Unseen, nay, the Invisible? Superstition gives its God a shape . . . but religion tells us that with Him, form and duration are not. (99)

Later, in *The Life of Sterling* (1851) we have a flesh-and-blood hero, Sterling, in the crises of a nineteenth-century career; and we have also the real Coleridge himself, all of Carlyle's ambiguities toward Coleridge resolved into a famous and devastating attack. Sterling had given himself over to radicalism:

> Piety of heart, a certain reality of religious faith, was always Sterling's, the gift of nature to him which he would not and could not throw away; but I find at this time his religion is as good as altogether Ethnic, Greekish, what Goethe calls the Heathen form of religion. The Church, with her articles, is without relation to him. And along with obsolete spiritualisms, he sees all-manner of obsolete thrones and big-wigged temporalities; and for them also can prophesy, and wish, only a speedy doom. (11:51)

But the young man comes under the spell of Coleridge. Coleridge

> thought to hold, he alone in England, the key of German and other Transcendentalisms; knew the sublime secret of believing by "the reason"

what "the understanding" had been obliged to fling out as incredible; and could still, after Hume and Voltaire had done their best and worst with him, profess himself an orthodox Christian. (11:53)

Carlyle finally rejects the Kantian duality: the mind is *one*, as Hamann had declared, contra Kant. "What the light of your mind, which is the direct inspiration of the Almighty, pronounces incredible,—that, in God's name, leave uncredited" (11:60). For all his brilliance, Coleridge is idle, irresolute, trifling. "Those dead Churches, this dead English Church especially, must be brought to life again . . . . But how, but how! By attending to the 'reason' of man, said Coleridge, and duly chaining up the 'understanding' of man: . . . it all turned upon these, if you could well understand them,—which you couldn't" (11:59). This is as much as to say that Coleridge can only pretend to revalidate outworn Anglicanism by "playing jesuitic tricks with his own convictions," by "putting-out the eyes of his mind." Coleridge would maintain "obsolete spiritualisms," "obsolete thrones and big-wigged temporalities."[13] Carlyle sees Sterling as a victim of the conflicting currents of the time and hence vulnerable to Coleridge's specious reasoning. In Carlyle's view Sterling was primarily a poet, and yet he was for a time ordained and a curate in the Church of England. He resigned his calling ostensibly for reasons of health, but Carlyle believes he regretted it on other grounds, this "clerical aberration" that was due to Coleridge.[14] The issue is a poignant one because Carlyle had great affection for this interesting and ingratiating young man.

Not even under that horrendous intensity of his mother's scrutiny would Carlyle juggle words to set religion on false grounds, not even for the Scotch Calvinism that he valued more than the Anglicanism that Coleridge resuscitates. Yet for a time, like Wotton, he had to "shroud up his heart in mystery," to dissemble, and the "duty of *not* breaking his mother's heart" lay heavy on him. In this strait came to him the appreciation of metaphor, a godsend vital both to his

13. Carlyle holds Coleridge responsible also for the Oxford Movement, the Puseyism that is "the dancing of the sheeted dead" (Preface to Emerson's *Essays* [London: James Fraser, 1841], p. xii). In conversation with Monckton Milnes, Carlyle said that Coleridge "had a whore of a soul, incapable of any continence, always pouring itself out, without any cue for reproduction" (quoted, by Ian Campbell, "Conversations with Carlyle: The Monckton Milnes Diaries, Part 2," in *Prose Studies* x (1986), p. 23.

14. Archdeacon Julius Hare had published a life of Sterling from the Anglican point of view, and Carlyle was instigated to write his own *Life of Sterling* to set the record straight.

intellectual well-being and to his relationship with his mother. He found he could speak to her of God, of Jesus, and of biblical events, giving her to understand Calvinist-literally what he understood Germano-aesthetical-metaphorically.[15] His father, who died in 1832, had a great oral style: "Never shall we again hear such speech as that was: The whole district knew of it; and laughed joyfully over it, not knowing how otherwise to express the feeling it gave them." Carlyle explains it: his father's talk was "full of metaphors (though he knew not what a metaphor was)."[16] He envisages his father, that is, as a primitive poet, performing the essential heroic task of culture making by his metaphors; his mother, by implication, belongs also to this naive phase.

Carlyle himself has passed by ordeal from the naive phase of making metaphor into the skeptical phase of the cycle that understands its figures *as* figures. He finds nevertheless that the figures so understood have greater rather than less spiritual significance. He acquires the habit of referring to the heroic metaphorical mode as "the ancient dialect": "To speak in the ancient dialect, we 'have forgotten God.'" This, from *Past and Present*, means that in the modern dialect "we have taken up the Fact of this Universe as it *is not*";[17] or, translating further, we have got a wrong understanding of our priorities. The "ancient dialect" is the mode of the poets, the myth-makers. Even when understood in our modern prosaical (demythologized) way, the metaphorical mode is more potent, condensed, and meaningful, more adequate therefore to our sense of how things are. It is the essence of *Sartor*. In this central passage, Teufelsdröckh speaks:

> "All Emblematic things are properly Clothes, thought-woven or hand-woven: must not the Imagination weave Garments, visible Bodies, wherein the *else invisible* [my emphasis] creations and inspirations of our Reason

15. Eric Bentley, in a book generally wrongheaded and dated, recognizes this strategy, quoting Grierson: "Are you [Carlyle] taking refuge from a decision in a cloud of words that would have one meaning for your mother and another for yourself?" (*A Century of Hero-Worship* [Philadelphia: Lippincott, 1944], p. 56). Herbert Grierson, in a lecture (published as a pamphlet) that hardly justifies his title, "Carlyle and Hitler" (Cambridge, England, 1933), said that Carlyle, "through regard for his old mother, . . . continued to use in a sense of his own the language to which she and he were accustomed" (p. 5). Grierson quotes Nietzsche's witty insight: "At bottom he is an English Atheist who makes it a point of honor not to be so."

16. "James Carlyle," in *Reminiscences*, ed. Charles Eliot Norton (London: Dent, 1972), pp. 2–3.

17. *Past and Present, Works* 10:136. See also Preface to Emerson's *Essays*, where he uses the variant "old dialects," p. xi.

are, like Spirits, revealed, and first become all-powerful. . . . Nay, if you consider it, what is Man himself, and his whole terrestrial Life, but an Emblem; a Clothing or visible Garment for that divine ME of his, cast hither, like a light-particle, down from Heaven? Thus is he said also to be clothed with a Body [this is an echo of Job 10:11]."

"Language is called the Garment of Thought: however, it should rather be, Language is the Flesh-Garment, the Body, of Thought."[18]

It has taken us generations to catch up to this prescient thought of Carlyle's that anticipates the contemporary theory that metaphor is essential to culture making and world making, to literature and also to ordinary life, to religion and even—it is now generally proposed as seldom heretofore—to philosophy and science.[19]

"I said that imagination wove this Flesh-Garment; and does not she? Metaphors are her stuff: examine Language; what, if you except some few primitive elements (of natural sound), what is it all but Metaphors, recognized as such, or no longer recognized; still fluid and florid, or now solid-grown and colourless? If those same primitive elements are the osseous fixtures in the Flesh-Garment, Language,—then are Metaphors its muscles and tissues and living integuments."

The Editor of *Sartor* interrupts, pretending to object to this outrageous argument—Carlyle's way of protecting himself and at the same time indicating that the ideas are radical and revolutionary:

Than which paragraph on Metaphors did the reader ever chance to see a more surprisingly metaphorical? However, that is not our chief grievance; the Professor continues:

"Why multiply instances? It is written, the Heavens and the Earth shall fade away like a Vesture [Psalm 102:25–26; Matthew 4:4]; which indeed they are: the Time-vesture of the Eternal. Whatsoever sensibly exists [apprehensible to our senses], whatsoever represents Spirit to Spirit, is properly a Clothing, a suit of Raiment, put on for a season, and to be laid off. Thus in this one pregnant subject of CLOTHES, rightly understood, is included all that men have thought, dreamed, done, and been: the whole External Universe and what it holds is but Clothing, and the essence of all Science lies in the PHILOSOPHY OF CLOTHES."[20]

Little did Carlyle know that his archenemy, the utilitarian philoso-

18. *Sartor*, p. 73.
19. George Lakoff and Mark Johnson, *Metaphors We Live By* (Chicago: Univ. of Chicago Press, 1980).
20. *Sartor*, pp. 73–74.

pher Jeremy Bentham, had elaborated the same position on the provisionality of language as "put on for a season, to be laid off." Bentham's *Theory of Fictions*, however, is dry reading and had to await C. K. Ogden's recognition.[21] But Carlyle's theory of fictions has been steadily accessible because it is in the accessible form of metaphors. "Than which paragraph on Metaphors did the reader ever chance to see a more surprisingly metaphorical?" Before Nietzsche, Carlyle "frolics in metaphors" and, before Nietzsche, envisages truth as a "mobile army of metaphors"; and of course, though his terms are a little more guarded, he had virtually, before Nietzsche, announced the Death of God.[22] Carlyle, before Nietzsche, recognizes Goethe's *Entsagen* and Novalis's *Selbsttödtung* as the renunciation of certainties, absolutes, dogmas, which renunciation must precede philosophic thinking.[23] Nietzsche and Carlyle had the same German sources, but Nietzsche may owe more to Carlyle than he cares to admit. He takes the trouble to repudiate Carlyle with malicious emphasis. His *Übermensch*, superman, has little to do with Carlyle's heroes, but his metaphor-fiction theory appears to owe something to Carlyle.

Carlyle's mother was extrapolated onto a host of mothers and other worthy pious literalists, whose faith should not be disturbed. There are occasional times when the doubleness of metaphor is not equal to the pressure, and Carlyle uses a kind of evasion: in the History of Literature that is really a History of Religion, he professes that "it is not our part to touch on sacred things, but. . . ." *But* "in another point of view"—the non-sacred-thing point of view, presumably, or the intellectually respectable point of view—Christianity is the reve-

21. C. K. Ogden wrote an introduction (of 152 pages) and selected passages for his edition of *Bentham's Theory of Fictions* (1932; reprint London: Routledge and Kegan Paul, 1951; Paterson, N.J.: Littlefield Adams, 1959). Ogden introduced Vaihinger to Bentham's theory, which complements Vaihinger's theory of fictions, while it reverses it, making language the means to the other fictions (Hans Vaihinger, *Die Philosophie des Als-Ob* [Berlin: Reither und Reichard, 1911]; trans. C. K. Ogden in consultation with Vaihinger, *The Philosophy of As If* [New York: Harcourt Brace, 1924]).

22. Some references to these elements of Nietzsche's thought may be found in Ronald Hayman, *Nietzsche: A Critical Life* (New York: Oxford Univ. Press, 1980), pp. 92, 163, 237, 238. Carlyle declares, "Divinity has withdrawn from the Earth" in "Characteristics" (1831), *Essays* 3:26.

23. *"Selbst-tödtung* had been happily accomplished; and my mind's eyes were now unsealed, and its hands ungyved" (*Sartor*, p. 186). See Georg Tennyson, *Sartor Called Resartus* (Princeton: Princeton Univ. Press, 1965), p. 315, for Carlyle's adjustment of Novalis. Compare Keats, born in the same year as Carlyle, working out the doctrine of "Negative Capability."

lation of eternity in time. "This truth, whatever may be the opinions we hold on Christian doctrines, or whether we hold upon them a sacred silence or not, we must recognize in Christianity" (67). "Sacred silence" is in fact a refusal to say whether one believes in a personal God and biblical miracles. The odd locution is useful again soon after in the Odin lecture, where he is sketching out the theory of Hero-Worship, the "transcendent admiration of a Great Man." "Is not that the germ of Christianity itself? The greatest of all Heroes is One— whom we do not name here! Let sacred silence meditate that sacred matter."[24] We have to observe that "silence" ranks high in the Carlylean scale of values in general: "Speech is silver, silence is golden."[25] At times it represents the magnificent paradox of Psalm 19: "The heavens *declare* the glory of God; and the firmament sheweth his handywork. Day unto day uttereth *speech*, and night unto night sheweth knowledge." Or in Addison's version: "The heavens are *telling*." But here "sacred silence" is Carlyle's ingenious way of remaining noncommittal, of sounding orthodox enough to the *mithers* of Scotland, and England; we know it means "I do not believe, but you can go on believing, and I respect your belief." The phenomenon marks the early, heroic phase of a culture, as with Old Testament writers; as with Carlyle's father using metaphors without knowing they are metaphors. Carlyle notes that Socrates, living in a phase of the cycle similar to his own, "shows a lingering kind of awe and attachment for the old religion of his country, and often we cannot make out whether he believed it or not." We can conclude that Carlyle deliberately cultivates Socratic ambiguity. It requires the greatest alertness and ingenuity in speech and writing; Socrates, he wryly observes, "must have had a painful intellectual life" (35). Carlyle's recourse to "sacred silence" epitomizes some of his own intellectual pain.

But the whole problem is triumphantly solved in *Sartor Resartus*, solved by the beautiful subterfuges of masks, of metaphors in the larger sense of fiction or myth and in the smaller sense of incidental figures—a style flashing with metaphors. *Wotton Reinfred* fails utterly; it is too painfully direct and transparent. How to say it? Say that Christianity is merely one myth among others, that Jesus was a mere man, that biblical miracles never happened? Have someone *else* say it:

24. *Heroes, Works* 5:11.
25. *Sartor*, pp. 218–19.

Diogenes Teufelsdröckh, *man* in all his ambiguity, both excrement of the devil and God-born, fallible, lovable, *worshipable* man. Have him say, in sum, that Christianity is a myth but that myths are infinitely precious survival systems for man in a phantasmagorical chaos of sensations; have him say that Jesus was a human being but that the sublimity of his preaching and the example of his life are instances of human potential before which, astounded, we must be struck with reverence; have him say that biblical miracles are fairy tales but symbols of infinite significance, signifying that man has recognized the mystery that his finite intelligence cannot master and has recognized the much greater miracles of being, of the sky above, and of the moral law within. Have him *introduced* by someone, an *Editor*, for the mission of an editor is to present everything objectively and, uncommitted, to become a personification, a metaphor for the *Entsagen*, the *Selbsttödtung*, the renunciation of certainties, the open mind. Let the Editor intrigue and implicate the reader with Swiftian, Sternian, Jean-Pauline games so that the reader is at least ready to *play* at foregoing his own certainties. Let the biography of Diogenes Teufelsdröckh be such that his anguish is proved on our pulses; and let his discovery of salvation through the whole German school come before the reader in the passionate imagistic metaphorical mode that can make otherwise difficult concepts at last accessible. Let his discovery come by means of a pretended *treatise*, a metaphor for the whole post-Kantian-Herderian-Schillerian-Goethean school of thought; and let that treatise be on *clothes*, the metaphor for all the varied, changing, wearing out, repaired, replaced, expendable, and provisional institutions of our culture, and the metaphor for culture itself as the society makes itself in it, and as man makes himself in his society, for the metaphors we live by, and for metaphors about metaphors. And let man be the *tailor*, *Sartor*, himself ever being patched, cobbled, remade, *retailored, Resartus*, the culturemaker remaking himself in his own culture. And let there be a game of teaching German, for teaching is painlessly done by games: and so let there be pretense to *translate* from Professor Teufelsdröckh's Clothes-Philosophy with the German frequently interpolated in parentheses after the translation. This will give vraisemblance to the pretense of translating; for the learned, moreover, it will explain the actual provenance of these German ideas and terms; for the hungry mind, it will be solid nourishment; the indolent can simply skip the German without losing the thread. So was performed a unique pedagogical service to a whole society that affected the thought of all contemporary writers (as George Eliot says), that was a survival manual for countless thinkers in crisis (as T. H. Green explains), that perhaps more than any other single volume changed the course of intellectual development in England, so that change— *Entwicklung*, development, becoming—became the ground of being, the metaphor of relativity by which, more or less, we still live and move.

Carlyle's mother died in 1853, when Carlyle was fifty-eight. I believe Carlyle's writings thereafter are not quite so guarded. I do not think there are any more "sacred silences," though there may still be some cagey noncommittals. But the great principles of metaphor—to which this pious mother had helped unknowingly to bring him— were now established as his own mode and the mode of salvation.

When Carlyle died, there was no religious service whatsoever except, apparently, some nonsectarian flowers on the coffin in that chilly gray November burial day in Ecclefechan. This was in accord with Scotch custom but seems particularly appropriate for Carlyle. For people asked and still ask, "What is Carlyle's religion anyway? Or does he have one?"[26] He was faithful, in his fashion, to the Enlightenment, to his own enfranchisement by the light of intellect from the old literalist supernaturalist Christianity he had been brought up in. But he discovered, with the help of the new German learning, something better, a way of understanding Judeo-Christian scriptures and all religions in general as metaphoric or symbolic embodiments of aspects of real human experience. This validates the old religion, moves it out of the privileged area into literature, into poetry, or into art and yet reveals it as much richer in meaning than the old fundamentalist reading allowed. But the *reductiveness* of the Enlightenment that dismisses religion as mere myth and its agents as quacks and charlatans, Carlyle deplored even more than narrow literalism and personal gods. His mother's way was a better way than Gibbon's and Hume's. But both, in their different ways, are reductive, terribly inadequate to the truth of human experience. Man is most properly engaged in Reverence, or Wonder.

And what are the objects of Reverence, or Wonder? Carlyle's "Natural Supernaturalism" could be called scientific supernaturalism, for it is a religion that does not offend the scientific mind.

26. These words are those of the philosopher E. E. Caird, quoted by Tennyson in *Sartor Called Resartus*, p. 18.

But Carlyle sounds "religious," and this misled people then and misleads them now for the reason that I have indicated—that he wanted to mislead some people. He found that by understanding the Bible as metaphor and by talking about religion in metaphors, he was able to let his mother think he still had his faith and yet present his own religion honestly. He perpetually preaches his humanism with metaphors drawn above all from the Bible. Emerson found Nature the great resource for metaphors, for symbols; it is so too for Carlyle (the heavens still declare the glory of God), but the Bible is a still greater resource. What does this mean? That it is *only* through religious and biblical (or literary) metaphor that we can express an adequate sense of man. The Germans from Herder and Hamann on appreciated Old Testament metaphor as man-made and as a marvel. The metaphor-making powers, such as statements about God and the "ancient dialect," may be man's most marvelous and most holy power. Without these, Carlyle would be a deist or an atheist. With them, religion is his perspective, his ground of being, his "chief fact."

6. Odin

When Carlyle used the term "Hero-Worship" in his lecture series title, it was not the commonplace it is today; its very newness suggested a new religion of humanism. We must note that it had been used by Hume in *The Natural History of Religion*, for its use is one indication of Hume's great influence on Carlyle's thought.[1] Carlyle, as we have observed above, had approved Hume's "natural-history"—or scientific—approach to religion but indicated Hume's error: Hume regards religion as a disease, and Carlyle regards it in the German fashion, as a proper human function, as health.[2] But it may be Hume's best insight and Carlyle's most notable borrowing to insist on the limits of human knowledge. *The Natural History of Religion* concludes: "The whole is a riddle, an enigma, an inexplicable mystery. Doubt, uncertainty, suspence of judgment appear the only result of our most accurate scrutiny concerning this subject."[3] Against the dogmatic arrogance of religionists, Carlyle insists on the mystery, just as Hume does, for the best of scientific reasons. Carlyle is by no means a mystic or a mystery-monger in any of his works. Like Max Müller he has learned the Kantian lesson; to consider how it is that man can believe he knows so much more than he *can* know. And so he addresses religious matters in this scientific manner, but with something Hume could not bring to the subject: a warm, wondering, human Herderian sympathy.

Heroes, then, begins with the two religious subjects, Odin, the Hero as Divinity, and Mahomet, the Hero as Prophet. Modern critics have had little to say on these. Some note that Odin is a very *odd* choice and

---

1. *The Natural History of Religion and Prologues Concerning Natural Religion*, ed. A. Wayne Colver and John Vladimir Price (Oxford: Clarendon Press, 1976), p. 45. The best edition of *Heroes* for annotation is the one edited by Archibald MacMechan (Boston: Ginn, 1901). But my page references to *Heroes* in this chapter are, as elsewhere, to volume 5 of the standard Edinburgh edition of the *Works*.
2. "Signs of the Times," *Essays* 2:76.
3. *The Natural History of Religion*, p. 95.

move quickly on to the more interesting lectures on human beings.[4]
But the opening lectures give essential framework to the whole and
constitute part of its meaning; they exhibit, moreover, a remarkable
virtuosity. Here in the opening of the Odin lecture Carlyle declares,

> A man's religion is the chief fact with regard to him . . . , the thing a man
> does practically believe (and this is often enough *without* asserting it even
> to himself, much less to others): the thing a man does practically lay to
> heart, and know for certain, concerning his vital relations to this myste-
> rious Universe, and his duty and destiny there, that is in all cases the
> primary thing for him, and creatively determines all the rest. (5:2, 3)

The whole *Heroes* book is about that "chief fact." At the beginning of
this first lecture the topic is announced as "illimitable," "wide as
Universal History itself." The hero is "a natural luminary shining by
the gift of Heaven"; to understand Heroism is to grasp "the divine
relation which in all times unites a Great Man to other men" (5:2).
This lecture is no mere excursus into Norse mythology.

The Odin lecture is in fact a sensational tour de force, as we shall
see, but it is also a study of Norse mythology, presented from
considerable reading and generally sound scholarship—except for, as
usual with Carlyle, the doubtful etymologies. He follows in the line of
Herder, who had urged the revival of Northern mythology. Scandinavian paganism, Carlyle says, is especially interesting to us because it
is the latest European paganism, lasting till the eleventh century, and
because it was the creed of our own forebears and has been preserved
so well. We know his sources with fair certainty.[5] First, he had Paul
Henri Mallet's *Northern Antiquities* (1770), translated from the
French by that hero of English Romanticism, Bishop Percy. There was
an Edinburgh reprint of this in 1809. Mallet uses the rich literary
records of the twelfth and thirteenth centuries, Saemund's *Elder, or
Poetic, Edda*, Snorri Sturluson's *Younger, or Prose, Edda*, and Saxo
Grammaticus's *Gesta Danorum*, all of which Carlyle mentions in the

---

4. For a recent example, see Charles H. Haws, "Carlyle's Concept of History in
Heroes and Hero-Worship," in *Thomas Carlyle 1981* (Papers given at the International
Thomas Carlyle Centenary Symposium at the University of Mainz), ed. Horst W.
Drescher (Frankfurt am Main: Peter Lang Verlag, 1983), pp. 153–64. "Carlyle's
selection of Odin to represent the Divine hero seems extreme, not because he failed to
select Buddha, Confucius or Christ, but because the historical basis for such a man/god
is weak" (p. 154).

5. See Herbert Wright, "The Sources of Carlyle's Lecture on 'The Hero as
Divinity,'" *Modern Language Review* 13 (1918):87–90.

lecture.[6] He had also Jakob Grimm's *Deutsche Mythologie* (1835) and the poet Ludwig Uhland's *Der Mythus von Thor nach nordischen Quellen* (1836). For the Odin material he seems to me to follow Mallet. "Grimm, the German Antiquary, goes so far as to deny that any man Odin ever existed," Carlyle says, but he insists that there must have been a real human Odin who later came to be considered a god—this point is very important for the humanist argument of the whole book. Mallet propounds this Euhemerist theory and recounts the exploits of the Odin who is said to have come north a few decades before the birth of Christ.[7] Carlyle dismisses Thomas Gray: Gray is to Norse lore as Pope is to Homer; but he acclaims Uhland's "fine essay on Thor" and uses it. The lecture is full of delight in this newly discovered great wealth of mythology; it broke ground; it did much to bring Norse material into fuller appreciation; and it inspired later poetry such as Arnold's "Balder Dead" and William Morris's *Sigurd the Volsung.*

But the lecture is much more than Norse mythology. A second pattern of significance can be discerned under the Norse material. As we imagine the lecture in that spring of 1840, the choice of Odin seems both a stunning coup de theatre and a well considered strategy. We imagine the run-of-the-mill lecturegoer's first reaction to "The Hero as Divinity"—Divinity? with a frisson of shock. But Jesus Christ is *the* example of divinity: how unorthodox to treat him as a *hero*—Ah, I see it is *Odin* as divinity—we will hear something new, of the Germans' mythology.

In fact that original shock was the appropriate reaction. For the whole lecture on Odin is in fact a disguised account of the nature of Christ and of the early development of Christianity, in terms as rationalist and non-supernaturalist as those of D. F. Strauss's *Leben Jesu* (1835–1836), which was being read and reviewed by the cognoscenti in England in 1838 and 1839.[8] Strauss applies the myth theory

6. To this list Hill Shine adds *Illustrations of Northern Antiquities* (1814), by H. W. Weber, R. Jamieson, and Walter Scott, which analyzes and translates from the *Heldenbuch* and *Niebelungenlied* (*Carlyle's Unfinished History of German Literature*, ed. Hill Shine [Lexington: Univ. of Kentucky Press, 1951], pp. xx, 16, 73).

7. K. J. Fielding tells us of his further reading: travel books on Iceland and Greenland and a translation of the nineteenth-century Swedish poet Esaias Tegnér's *Frithiof's Saga* ("Carlyle and Esaias Tegnér," *Carlyle Newsletter 5* [Spring 1984]: 3–10, 35).

8. See Carlyle's letter to Emerson, 7 November 1839, and Sterling's to Carlyle, 30 June 1839 (in forthcoming volumes of Carlyle's *Letters*). See also William Allingham's

to the life of Jesus, denies the historical basis of supernatural elements in the Gospels, and assigns them to an unintentionally creative legend (the "myth") developed between the death of Jesus and the writing of the Gospels. So the Odin lecture is a declaration that Christianity does not depend on supernatural manifestations and has great worth that withstands and survives Enlightenment reductionism.

"The Hero as Divinity—Odin," concerns the "oldest primary form of Heroism" and can be read to refer all the way through to Jesus. He that hath ears to hear, let him hear. This paganism—that is, super-naturalism—is a strange-looking thing these days, Carlyle says, "almost inconceivable to us. . . . A bewildering, inextricable jungle of delusions, confusions, falsehoods and absurdities covering the whole field of life." We are filled with astonishment, "Almost, if it were possible, with incredulity. . . . That men should have worshipped their poor fellow-man as a God . . . and fashioned for themselves such a distracted chaos of hallucinations by way of Theory of the Universe: all this looks like an incredible fable. . . . Nevertheless it is a clear fact that they did it. . . . This is strange." Yet, "such things were and are in man; in all men; in us too" (5:4). We see here the experiential approach, like that of William James. Religious experiences are our facts. They are, Carlyle would say, emblems of man's infinite capacity. And so pagan religion (let us continue to read *Christianity*) is not "mere quackery, priestcraft, and dupery." Paganism and all other *isms* "have all had a truth in them, or men would not have taken them up" (5:4). He calls Christianity *Christianism* to enforce the parallel here. In the comparative way he cites the "Lama-ism" of Tibet as another form of our need for a "greatest" man to revere.

There is a theory, he says, that these things are all allegory, "a play

---

Diary, 1824–1889, ed. H. Allingham and D. Radford (Harmondsworth, England: Penguin, 1985) for Carlyle's retrospective remark of 1872 on Strauss: "What all wise men had had in their minds for fifty years past, and thought it fittest to hold their peace about."

Ian Campbell has recently brought to light some wonderful Carlyle conversation ("Conversations with Carlyle: The Monckton Milnes Diaries, Part 1," *Prose Studies* 8 [1985]: 45–57) that as he says gives us "a real advance in understanding" (p. 55), for it is unbuttoned talk, incited by the pleasure of Milnes's company. This remark seems to me to capture Carlyle's sense of the humanity of Jesus: "I would rather have one real glimpse of the young Jew face of Christ than see all the Raffaels in the world" (quoted by Campbell, p. 51). His religious historicism is particularly clear in another remark: Some day "people will look on our Xtianity much as we look on Paganism" (p. 53).

of poetic minds," a "shadowing-forth . . . in personification and visual forms, of what [is] known and felt of this Universe. . . . What a man feels intensely, he struggles to speak-out of him . . . in visual shape . . . as if with a kind of life" (5:5). But the allegory theorists do not have the whole secret, though they are on the way toward truth. The fact is the allegories cannot *precede* the belief. The belief must be there. And there was belief in the "miracle" of Nature and the Universe, "beautiful, awful, unspeakable." "Hardened round us, encasing wholly every notion we form, is a wrappage of traditions, hearsays, mere words. We call that fire of the black thunder-cloud 'electricity' and lecture learnedly about it" (5:8)—and we forget the marvel and unknown of it. In Odin's time there were no "hearsays" to chain up experience, and so men were open to worship of the transcendent unknown.

> Science has done much for us; but it is a poor science that would hide from us the great deep sacred infinitude of Nescience. . . . That great mystery of *Time*, were there no other . . . on which we and all the Universe swim like exhalations. . . . This Universe . . . a Force . . . a Force which is *not* *we*. . . . In such a time as ours it requires a Prophet or Poet to teach us, namely, the stripping-off of those poor undevout wrappages, nomenclatures and scientific hearsays,—this, the ancient earnest soul, as yet unencumbered with these things, did for itself. . . . All was Godlike or God. . . . But now if all things whatsoever that we look upon are emblems to us of the Highest God, I add that more so than any of them is man such an emblem. You have heard of St. Chrysostom's celebrated saying in reference to the Shekinah, or Ark of the Testimony, visible Revelation of God, among the Hebrews: "The true Shekinah is Man!" . . . we are the miracle of miracles,—the great inscrutable mystery of God. (5:8–10)

Spinoza too said something like this. But Carlyle finds it prudent to cite the saint, not Spinoza, teacher of the Germans, whose name carried still an aura of fearful heterodoxy. He continues in Herderian historicist vein: "The young generations of the world, who had in them the freshness of young children, and yet the depth of earnest men, who did not think they had finished-off all things in Heaven and Earth by merely giving them scientific names . . . they felt better what of divinity is in man and Nature" (5:11). If there was meaning even in the worship of a star, how much more in the case of a man!

> Hero-worship, heartfelt prostrate admiration, submission, burning, boundless, for a noblest godlike Form of Man,—is not that the germ of

Christianity itself? The greatest of all Heroes is One—whom we do not name here! Let sacred silence meditate that sacred matter; you will find it the ultimate perfection of a principle extant throughout man's whole history on earth. (5:11)

By his "sacred silence" Carlyle can avoid committing himself on the divinity of Christ, and at the same time he invites meditation—he that hath ears to hear, let him hear—and invites some to recognize that Christ is the subject of this lecture. The bold scheme of *Heroes* is essentially that the sacred and secular are all one—our reverence for Dante, Shakespeare, Johnson, Luther, Calvin, Napoleon, Cromwell is one with our reverence for Mahomet the prophet and for Odin/ Christ—"from Norse Odin to English Samuel Johnson, from the divine Founder of Christianity to the withered Pontiff of Encyclopedism [Voltaire, that is], in all times and places" (5:15). In fact, Carlyle's taking a "god" as hero is in itself the bold step and a clear statement against supernaturalism.

In old paganism, then, Carlyle finds "truth, only under an ancient obsolete vesture, but the spirit of it is still true" (5:15); *vesture* recalls *Sartor*, and the principle applies equally to Christianity. These Norse poems "have a *truth* in them, an inward perennial truth and greatness,—as, indeed, all must have that can very long preserve itself by tradition alone [read Christianity]. . . . They seem to have seen . . . what Meditation has taught all men in all ages, that this world is after all but a show,—a phenomenon or appearance, no real thing. All deep souls see into that,—the Hindoo Mythologist [mentioned several times in this comparative study of Odin], the German Philosopher [he means Kant and his Phenomena],—the Shakespeare—[and he quotes a favorite text:] 'We are such stuff as Dreams are made on!'" (5:36). This text captures for Carlyle his sense of metaphor—dream-stuff, *un*reality, and yet the most real thing that makes ourselves and our societies. The Norse mythology is marked, he continues, by "impersonation of the visible workings of Nature" (figures and metaphors, characteristic of scriptures, we add) that are "simple recognition of . . . Nature as a thing wholly miraculous, stupendous and divine."

In his panorama of Norse mythology, he likes especially the idea of the tree Igdrasil, with

roots deep-down in the kingdoms of Hela or Death; its trunk . . . heaven-high, . . . At the foot of it sit Three *Nornas*, Fates,—the Past, Present, Future. . . . Its "boughs," with their buddings and disleafings,—events, things suffered, things done, catastrophes,—stretch through all lands and times. Is not every leaf of it a biography, every fibre there an act or word? Its boughs are Histories of Nations. The rustle of it is the noise of Human Existence, onwards from an old. . . . Considering how human things circulate, each inextricably in communion with all,—how the word I speak to you today is borrowed, not from Ulfila the Moesogoth only, but from all men since the first man began to speak,—I find no similitude so true as this of a Tree. . . . The "*Machine* of the Universe,"—alas, do but think of that in contrast! (5:20–21)

Carlyle knows the surpassing shaping power of our radical metaphors. And he recognizes in this wonderful metaphor an early Germanic intimation of Herder's Historicism; in Carlyle's sense of "how human things circulate" we see another version of *Sartor's* "Organic Filaments" and the "living literal communion of Saints, the cloud of witness, wide as the World itself, and as the History of the World." We see also what Herder called *die Kette der Bildung*: the chain of culture. The most impressive thing of all is that this magnificent metaphor is the work of *man*. And that *man* is Odin, the "first Norseman who had an original power of thinking" (what Hamann called the poet at the beginning of days). "Existence has become articulate, melodious by him; he first made Life alive. . . . His view of the Universe once promulgated, a like view starts into being in all minds" (5:22)—such is the power of the creative metaphor. Carlyle pauses to note that the mythology is not a coherent *system* but rather a layered, shifting, accumulative *development*. (In this way, we know, he thinks of all religions, including Christianity.)

"How the man Odin came to be considered a *god*, the chief god" (5:24–25)—that is the question. Part of the Odin lore that Carlyle might have known is the account in one of the verse *Eddas* of how Odin was hanged on the Ash Tree, wounded, in order to learn the great secret of the runes of wisdom. Some mythographers consider the development of this aspect of the Odin material to be not merely a parallel to the Crucifixion but actually an effect of the influence of Christianity. But all we need note is the parallel, which might have given Carlyle the idea for the lecture. But the point about his account of Odin's apotheosis from man to god is that it is written with great passion precisely because it is written about Jesus.

People knew no limits to their admiration. . . . Fancy your own generous heart's-love of some greatest man expanding till it *transcended* all bounds,

till it filled and overflowed the whole field of your thought! Or what if this
man Odin,—since a great deep soul, with the afflatus and mysterious tide of
vision and impulse rushing on him he knows not whence, is ever an
enigma, a kind of terror and wonder to himself,—should have felt that
perhaps *he* was divine. . . . He was not necessarily false; he was but
mistaken, speaking the truest he knew [this state of mind had been
ascribed by rationalists to Jesus]. . . . And then consider what mere Time
will do in such cases; how if a man was great while living, he becomes
tenfold greater when dead. . . . Why, in thirty or forty years [the period
between the Crucifixion and the Gospels], were there no books, any great
man would grow *mythic*, the contemporaries who had seen him, being
once all dead. And in three-hundred years, and in three-thousand years!
(5:25–26)

Well, he means in eighteen hundred years. Our needs and wishes
shape our perceptions: "Curious to think how, for every man, any the
truest fact is modelled by the nature of man!"—even number (here is
Carlyle the mathematician): "The number *Twelve*, divisiblest of all,
which could be halved, quartered, parted into three, into six, the most
remarkable number,—this was enough to determine the *Signs of the
Zodiac*, the number of Odin's *Sons*, and innumerable other Twelves"
(5:26). It would be a slow mind that would not leap to think of twelve
tribes of Israel and twelve apostles and recognize that Carlyle is
implying the mythic elements in the Judeo-Christian tradition.

Carlyle envisages development in religions: paganism recognizes
Nature; the "recognition of Man and his Moral Duty . . . comes to
be the chief element only in purer forms of religion." Standard
historicist thought considers Christianity to be more developed in this
way than paganism and Judaism, and yet still only one religion among
others, to give way in time to another. And so Carlyle is very much
struck to find in the Igdrasil image, in Norse myth itself, the very idea
of cyclicism, and to find it still more conspicuous in the "old,
prophetic idea" of the "*Ragnarök*, consummation, or *Twilight of the
Gods.*"

The old Universe with its Gods is sunk; but it is not final death: there is to
be a new Heaven and a new Earth; a higher supreme God, and Justice to
reign among men. Curious: this law of mutation, which also is a law
written in man's inmost thought, had been deciphered by these old earnest
Thinkers in their rude style; and how, though all dies, and even gods die,
yet all death is but a phoenix fire-death, and new-birth into the Greater and

the Better! It is the fundamental Law of Being for a creature made of Time, living in this Place of Hope. (5:39)

Curious, he is saying, that these old earnest thinkers anticipate cyclic Historicism. The myth itself affords its own self-cancellation, what he himself had described in *Sartor* with his figure of the Phoenix-death-and-rebirth.

In conclusion he tells the touching story that belongs to the category folklorists call the heavenly visitor: King Olaf has been zealous in promulgating Christianity. As he is sailing along the shore of Norway, at a certain haven there steps into his ship

> a stranger, of grave eyes and aspect, red beard, of stately robust figure. . . . The courtiers address him; his answers surprise by their pertinency and depth: at length he is brought to the King. . . . As they sail along the beautiful shore . . . he addresses King Olaf thus: "Yes . . . it is all beautiful, with the sun shining on it there; green, fruitful, a right fair home for you; and many a sore day had Thor, many a wild fight with the rock Jötuns, before he could make it so. And now you seem minded to put away Thor. King Olaf, have a care!" said the stranger, drawing-down his brows;—and when they looked again, he was nowhere to be found.— This is the last appearance of Thor on the stage of this world! (5:40)

This is as though to say: Have a care, you Saint-Simonians, Comtists, Benthamites, Utilitarians, atheists, scientists, lest you put away Christianity! It is all beautiful, this great European cultural shore, and many a sore day had Christianity to make this tradition we live in and profit by. On Thor's apparition, Carlyle continues, "Do we not see well enough how the Fable might arise, without unveracity on the part of any one? It is the way most Gods have come to appear among men: thus, if in Pindar's time, 'Neptune was seen once at the Nemean Games,' what was this Neptune too but a 'stranger of noble grave aspect'" (5:40). And we call to mind some other visitors, the three mysterious "men" who appeared to Abraham in the plains of Mamre as he sat in the tent door in the heat of the day; or the stranger who appeared to the disciples on the road to Emmaus. These things are recorded "without unveracity" and are full of significance, just as this little story of Thor and King Olaf is full of significance. It is a beautiful metaphor for Carlyle's sense of the cyclical in history and for his sense of the invaluable humanity that exists in each religion and culture, each a unique and invaluable *Vorstellungsart* of man's spirituality. He concludes the lecture with the *Wilhelm Meister* passage he loves: "'To which of these Three Religions do you specially adhere?' inquires Meister of his Teacher. 'To all the Three!' answers the other, 'To all the Three'" (5:41).

This reading of the Odin lecture enhances both its discretion and its artistry. Carlyle's strategy of the bi-level meanings seems to have been widely successful: that is, readers are divided into two distinct classes—those who understand it as orthodox, and those who see the doubleness. One immediate reaction appeared in the first number of a Catholic paper, *The Tablet*.[9] Its founder Frederick Lucas, ex-Quaker, Roman Catholic convert, reported the Odin lecture at the time it was given. This report is of great interest for its immediacy: we can learn something of how the lecture sounded, as distinguished from the carefully revised version Carlyle published somewhat later. The essentials are the same. Lucas writes: "We have great pleasure in being able to lay before our readers a report which . . . may give them some notion . . . of the lectures of this extraordinary writer." He warns his Catholic readers that Carlyle is a "staunch Protestant" and therefore the journal dissents from his opinions. But Carlyle has

> a rare sincerity of heart and understanding, an utter inability to reconcile himself to anything but what appears to him to be truth. . . . Honour to Mr. Carlyle for what he has done. . . . It is of the utmost importance that we should be acquainted with every phase of the present revival of spiritual life in England, and we may be sure . . . that the writings of Mr. Carlyle are not the least pregnant phenomenon. If in anything he is blind, it is the blindness of a Sampson, who, at one stoop, brings down the temple of the Philistines—the Benthamites and Utilitarians. . . . More than one person, we know well, owes him an incalculable debt of gratitude for the guidance his writings have afforded to the precincts of the true faith.

Now, the appreciation of this "sincerity" and "true faith" may be received a little ironically. Lucas proceeds to give a long summary that is nowhere at odds with the published version; but it ignores, of course, the subtextual comments on Christianity that I have discerned.

The learned John Tulloch, author of *Movements of Religious*

---

9. I am indebted to the kindness and insight of K. J. Fielding for this item (private communication).

Thought in Britain in the Nineteenth Century (1885),[10] knows his own orthodoxy enough to deplore Carlyle's rejection of miracle yet says "he was great as a Moral Teacher in so far as he preserved certain elements of his early creed."[11] But the "creed" is precisely what Carlyle rejects; he preserves the ethics and the attitude of reverence. Tulloch deplores Matthew Arnold's non-supernaturalist position much more than Carlyle's, but in fact they are the same. Carlyle's is only more guarded, more veiled in expression. R. H. Hutton, a literary critic of an orthodox Christian persuasion, makes Arnold out to be the villain of infidelity, not recognizing that Carlyle had said it all first.[12] More surprising is the fact that H. D. Trail, editor of the Centenary edition of Carlyle, misses the point of the Odin lecture completely: "No judicious lecturer" could have chosen the subject; it has "an almost ludicrous effect" and is "purely fantastic" but "eminently simple"![13] And it is even more surprising to find C. F. Harrold, for all his wide and sympathetic Carlyle scholarship, still referring to Carlyle's "fundamentally orthodox position"![14] All these commentators must be classed as more or less in the category of *protected mithers.*

The ones who see through the doubleness come from a wide spectrum. William Thomason, later archbishop of York, reviewed

10. *Movements of Religious Thought in Britain in the Nineteenth Century* (London: Longmans, 1885; reprint with an introduction by A. C. Cheyne, New York: Humanities Press, 1971), chap. 5, "Thomas Carlyle as a Religious Teacher," pp. 169–208.

11. *Movements of Religious Thought*, p. 206.

12. *Essays in Some of the Modern Guides of English Thought in Matters of Faith* (London: Macmillan, 1887), p. 130.

13. *Works* 5:viii–ix, quoted by K. J. Fielding in "Carlyle and Esaias Tegnér," *Carlyle Newsletter* 5 (Spring 1984):10.

14. *Carlyle and German Thought: 1819–1839* (1934; reprint, London: Anchor Books, 1963), p. 18. David DeLaura gathers a valuable collection of early recognitions of Carlyle's heterodoxy and then makes a fresh exploration into the Carlylean elements retained in Arnold's thought despite Arnold's frequent disclaimers—a field to which DeLaura has already made such a signal contribution ("Carlyle and Arnold: The Religious Issue," in *Carlyle Past and Present*, ed. K. J. Fielding and Rodger L. Tarr [New York: Barnes and Noble, 1976], pp. 127–54. The earlier essay is "Arnold and Carlyle," *PMLA* 79 [March 1964]:104–29). But DeLaura remains remarkably unsympathetic to both Carlyle's and Arnold's concern with other religions. "Despite Arnold's early interest in Eastern religions," he writes, "and Carlyle's flirtations with the German Idealists, both remained intellectually and emotionally what the categorizers call 'ethical monotheists'" (p. 135). But Arnold's interest in Eastern religions was not simply "early" and is hardly at odds with "ethical monotheism"; "flirtations" simply shows a failure to understand a momentous intellectual exchange.

Heroes for the *Christian Remembrancer*, and although he hasn't the faintest idea what is going on in the Odin lecture—Odin, Mahomet, "Such a menagerie!"—he deduces on other grounds very unequivocally that *Heroes* "is not a Christian book."[15] The liberal Anglican F. D. Maurice answered this review with a defense of Carlyle as Christian, but—as sometimes happens with Maurice—the reasoning is not very strong.[16] Froude seems to understand: he remarks dryly that Odin was the example of hero as god, "Odin, and not Another, for obvious reasons";[17] and he shows elsewhere a clear understanding of Carlyle's qualified Christianity.[18] William Ewart Gladstone perceives on reading Froude's biography of Carlyle, "When he writes to his mother he assumes the phraseology of a Christian. . . . This is not hypocrisy but it is fiction; it is deception, beginning probably in self-deception. He could not bear to give pain to his mother he dearly and deeply loved."[19] The Roman Catholic William Barry understands his relation to orthodoxy:

> Carlyle, true messenger from the Ideal though I hold him to be, took away from the sum of religious knowledge more than he brought to it. This great and whole spirit did not know Christ. . . . In his Bible there was no New Testament. . . . Carlyle disliked Strauss, and spoke of Renan with loathing; but in the sum of the matter he cannot have been at issue with them. Their Christ was a myth, and so was his.[20]

The French critic Victor Basch writes, "Basically, he professed a deism which was not so far as he thought from that of Voltaire. But his deism was exalted by the great wings of poetry."[21] Great wings of metaphor, we may say. But it is theism if not Deism itself. Herbert Grierson asserts that Carlyle left Christianity early and completely, but "through regard for his old mother he continued to use in a sense of his own the language to which she and he were accustomed, with an

---

15. *Christian Remembrancer* 6 (August 1843): 121–43; reprinted in *Thomas Carlyle, The Critical Heritage*, ed. Jules Paul Seigel (London: Routledge and Kegan Paul, 1971), pp. 177, 186.

16. *Critical Heritage*, pp. 193–207.

17. *Froude's Life of Carlyle*, abridged and ed. John Clubbe (Columbus: Ohio Univ. Press, 1979), p. 389.

18. *Froude's Life*, pp. 567–70.

19. Quoted by Fred Kaplan, *Thomas Carlyle: A Biography* (Ithaca: Cornell Univ. Press, 1983), p. 332.

20. *Heralds of Revolt* (London: Hodder and Stoughton, 1904), pp. 73, 86.

21. *Carlyle, l'homme et l'oeuvre* (Paris: Gallimard, 1938), p. 254.

effect that sometimes bewildered his readers, sometimes perhaps himself."[22]

The least sympathetic view is Eric Bentley's in *A Century of Hero-Worship*, a belated piece of the Lytton-Strachey Victorian-debunking school.[23] It was written in 1944, however, when Carlyle-bashing was in order because he was felt to underwrite Nazism. Bentley writes, "Carlyle avoids discussing the tenets of the faith ('it is not our part to touch on sacred things'). . . . The cries of '*Wer darf Ihn nennen?*' are the more vehement because they are the means by which he concealed himself from himself."[24] Bentley is amused that *Heroes* was for so long a school text. "The textbook editors have made a mistake if they think *Heroes* is Christian."[25] And he quotes Nietzsche on the subject, who called Carlyle both a fool and a dishonest atheist who never had the courage to avow his skepticism. "Carlyle overstressed religion in order to hide the shocking fact that he did not believe in religion, hard as he might try. . . . At bottom he is an English atheist who makes it a point of honor not to be so."[26] Matthew Arnold understood perfectly and granted that a religion such as Carlyle's was legitimate and in fact compatible with Anglicanism (which Carlyle did *not* believe). Arnold himself tells the story recounted in the Odin lecture, but without Odin, in *God and the Bible*, anticipating, as does Carlyle, our modern demythologizing school of biblical criticism.

The Odin lecture was—perhaps still may be—a fine piece of education: it expands the English consciousness to include the whole new cultural wealth of Northern mythology, in the main accurately and invitingly presented. It invites meditation on literature and religion, on their relationship, and on man and his metaphor makings. It is an Everlasting Nay to reductionism. It opens up the ground for the humane study of Comparative Religions—even for that landmark of Max Müller's, his lectures of 1870, *Introduction to the Science of Religion*. Max Müller writes:

> It is impossible to express abstract ideas except by metaphor, and it is not too much to say that the whole dictionary of ancient religions is made up of metaphors. . . . We shall no longer try to force a literal sense of words

22. "Carlyle and Hitler" (Cambridge, 1933), p. 5.
23. *A Century of Hero-Worship* (Philadelphia: Lippincott, 1944), p. 18.
24. Bentley, p. 39.
25. Bentley, p. 59.
26. Quoted by Bentley, pp. 59, 60.

which, if interpreted literally, must lose their true and original purport; we shall no longer interpret the Law and the Prophets as if they had been written in the English of our own century, but read them in a truly historic spirit, prepared for the many difficulties, undismayed by many contradictions, which, so far from disproving the authenticity, become . . . the strongest confirmatory evidence of the age, the genuineness, and the real truth of ancient sacred books.[27]

For Max Müller these ancient sacred books include the Indian ones that he edited, and he has his own Goethean way of adhering to all the great religions. The breadth of his religious interests and religious adherences leads him to this insight on metaphor, which Carlyle anticipates. In *Sartor Resartus* Carlyle exploits a fiction, or complex of metaphors, by which he protects himself and, protected, is able to say a thousand bold and new things. In this Hero-as-God lecture he protects himself with another fiction, or metaphor—Odin for Christ. Basil Willey says that he "possessed a power of double-vision,"[28] and I think this suggests his artistic power: in searching to explain the one thing in terms of another, he discovers real processes of religious phenomena in both and finds his way toward Comparative Religion. He demonstrates pattern in the great rich various plenitude of the creative human psyche. The Odin lecture is a substantial contribution to the "Natural History" of Religion. It has, I believe, a distinct link with Strauss's *Leben Jesu*. And in Strauss is also to be found the key idea of *Heroes*: Strauss venerates all religions but finds Christianity to be the "sublimest," identical with "the deepest philosophical truth." This truth is the idea of "perpetual incarnation." He proclaims the "divinely human."[29] George Eliot's translation of the *Leben Jesu* came out in 1848; but some of its ideas were already flourishing on British soil.

27. *Introduction to the Science of Religion* (London: Longmans, 1893), pp. 196–97.

28. *Nineteenth-Century Studies* (London: Chatto and Windus, 1949), p. 122.

29. See the "Concluding Dissertation" of David Friedrich Strauss's *Das Leben Jesu*, in the translation from the German by George Eliot (1848; 4th ed. London: Swan Sonnenschein, 1902), pp. 757–84. Particularly Carlylean ideas: "Christ . . . a hero" (p. 767); "the history of Christ . . . is a beautiful, sacred poem of the human race" (p. 776); "By faith in this Christ . . . , that is, by kindling within him the idea of Humanity, the individual man participates in the divinely human life of the species" (p. 780); "we have outgrown the notion, that the divine omnipotence is more completely manifested in the interruption of the order of nature than in its preservation" (p. 781).

Anthony J. Harding also quotes and discusses this work in "Sterling, Carlyle, and German Higher Criticism," *Victorian Studies* 26, no. 3 (Spring 1983): 269–86.

7. Mahomet, or Leaning to the East

Nord und West und Süd zersplittern
Throne bersten, Reiche zittern,
Flüchte du, im reinen Osten
Patriarchenluft zu kosten,
Unter Lieben, Trinken, Singen
Soll dich Chisers Quell verjüngen.

Dort, im Reinen und im Rechten,
Will ich menschlichen Geschlechten
In des Ursprungs Tiefe dringen
Wo sie noch von Gott empfingen
Himmelslehr' in Erdesprachen
Und sich nicht den Kopf zerbrachen.

—"Hegire"

Goethe the many-sided, having developed his powers in prodigious extent and depth, having accomplished everything, yet proceeded to exemplify in his old age the perpetual becoming, *Bildung*, and made yet again something new, publishing when he was seventy years old the *West-östlicher Diwan*, acknowledged as his finest lyric poetry.[1] Carlyle had a standard for poetry, a touchstone as a later critic would call it, in the incomparable lyrics of the Bible; he cites it on the rare occasions when he gives the accolade, to Dante, to Shakespeare (5:95, 111), and to this late poetry of Goethe, "which, for pregnancy and

1. *Goethes Werke*, ed. Erich Trunz (Hamburg: Christian Wegner Verlag, 1949), 2:7. The epigraph to this chapter gives the first two stanzas of seven.

North and West and South are cracking,
Thrones are toppling, empires shaking:
Flee thou to the veritable East
To try the air of the Patriarchs.
With loving, drinking, singing
Chiser's source will make thee young.

There at first hand and rightly
Will I search out the ancient origins
Of the human race,
In the place where they from God received
Heaven's lore in speech of earth,
The way it suits human capacity.

Goethe's own notes on the poem are in 2:552–53.

87

genial significance, except in the Hebrew Scriptures, you will nowhere match."[2] The *Diwan* begins with a "Hegire," the poet's flight from a Europe ravaged by the Napoleonic wars, to the romantic East, to love, to wine, to song, and to renewal in Chiser's spring of life. Goethe identifies himself with the great fourteenth-century Persian poet Hafiz, and indeed he is sometimes called "the German Hafiz."[3] Chiser, the guardian of the well of life, is said to have presented Hafiz with a flowing beaker, which drink bestowed on him the poet's consecration and undying fame.

In the East, the poet will seek out the deep origin of the human race, in that place where men still received from God "Himmelslehr' in Erdesprachen," the wisdom of heaven in the speech of earth, without racking their brains—effortlessly, that is, or naturally. Goethe's great figure, *Himmelslehr' in Erdesprachen*, could be taken as the inspiration for the whole operation of German Orientalism, arising from an appreciation of the figurativeness of the Hebrew poetry in the Bible and extending to the study of the languages, literatures, and cultures of the East, the birthplace of poetry and of religions. *Erdesprachen*, the human speech mode, is the mode of metaphor; through images we understand immediately, without racking our brains; through images the otherwise ineffable *Himmelslehre* is communicated.[4] God speaks, as the rabbis claim, in the language of men. And so *Erdesprachen* suggests poetry itself, and poetry as metaphor; it also suggests the metaphorical—as opposed to the literal—reading of the Bible. Goethe's "Hegire" can be understood in his own career as a flight to the Orient for inspiration—of a book of incomparable poetry; and it can also be understood as it is in Mahomet's career, as the mark of a new epoch in history.

Carlyle's Mahomet lecture comes out of this German Orientalism that Goethe epitomizes and that signifies a radical change from the old European attitude to the East. The European encounter with Islam is an extraordinary romantic tale where each phase leaves Western culture strangely touched and enriched. We would all be much poorer without the Moorish heritage of Spain; the cultural

2. "Goethe's Works," *Essays* 2:431. Textual references to *Heroes* in this chapter are to volume 5 of the *Works*.

3. By Carlyle, for one. "Death of Goethe," *Essays* 2:380.

4. Matthew Arnold took over this idea. Semitic people, he says, *orientalize*, that is, they speak in figures (*Collected Prose Works*, ed. R. H. Super, 11 vols. [Ann Arbor: Univ. of Michigan Press, 1960–1977], 6:22).

advantages of the Crusades are elaborated even in school history books; we have Morris (Moorish) dances in England, flamenco music in Spain and Los Angeles, a superb arithmetic system, a long medical tradition, FitzGerald's *Omar Khayyam*, Burton's *Arabian Nights*, and a thousand and one other treasures. But recognition of Islam came very late: in medieval times it was the great enemy of all Europe, and Mahomet was Antichrist or the devil. Islam was a handy epithet for one's enemy in religious wars—both Roman Catholics and Protestants applied it to one another. Some degree of learning about Islam was held to be necessary just in order to combat it. Pope Pius II, called Aeneas Silvius or Piccolomini (1405–1464), labored over a long scholarly letter to Mohammed the Conqueror to persuade him and his empire to recognize the errors of Islam and convert to Christianity. The effort was unusual, but the attitude was typical and longstanding. The Reformation changed attitudes somewhat: both Mahomet and Luther were after all reformers of an idolatrous Christianity.

The Renaissance produced certain heroes of cultural exchange, such as Edward Pocock (1604–1691), who learned Arabic at Oxford, published the Syriac version of the New Testament, lived for some time at Constantinople as chaplain to the British embassy and at Aleppo as chaplain to the English "Turkey Merchants," where he was friendly with learned Muslims and Jews; he collected manuscripts that became part of England's national treasure. Then there was Grotius, the great Dutch humanist whose invention of the idea of international law is a clue to his larger idea of religion. In his Mahomet lecture Carlyle gives a witty redaction of how Edward Pocock and Grotius meet in 1640 in Paris. These two *doctissimi* agree in rejecting as a vile canard the account of the "pigeon, trained to pick peas from Mahomet's ear and pass for an angel dictating to him."[5] Once more in our time, says Carlyle, "it is really time to dismiss all that" (5:44). He mentions a mediocre 1649 translation of the Koran into English (from a mediocre French version) and a polemical life of Mahomet written in 1697 by Humphrey Prideaux, *The True Nature of Imposture Fully Displayed in the Life of Mahomet* (5:65).

A change of direction came with George Sale (1697–1736), whose learning of Arabic was originally supported by the Society for the

5. Archibald MacMechan in his edition of *Heroes and Hero-Worship* (Boston: Ginn, 1901) gives the source in a note: *Specimen Historiae Arabum; Auctore Edvardo Pocockio*, ed. Joseph White (Oxford, 1806), pp. 191f.

Promotion of Christian Knowledge. The Society undertook to print a New Testament in Arabic for Syrian Christians; and Sale, who was active in the Society and a friend of John Wesley and Sir Hans Sloane, was the chief translator. In 1734 he published his excellent translation of the Koran; he used the Arabic commentaries and prefaced the whole with a "Preliminary Discourse" that remains valuable still as an account (to use his titles) "Of the Arabs before Muhammad . . . , their History, Religion, Learning and Customs . . . , Of the State of Christianity, particularly of the Eastern Churches, and of Judaism, at the time of Muhammad's Appearance," besides the life of Mahomet, and the subsequent history of Islam.[6] This was all translated early and diffused widely. It was used by Herder for his chapters on the Arabs in the *Ideen*;[7] it was the source for most Orientalist poetic works, such as Victor Hugo's; it was Carlyle's main source—he mentions Sale several times in the lecture (5:48, 64, 69). Sale diagnoses the Christian prejudice against Mahomet and explains how unjust it is. Gibbon calls him "our honest and learned translator . . . half a Musselmann."[8] The Society for the Promotion of Christian Knowledge came to have doubts, it is said, of Sale's Christian orthodoxy.

Meanwhile the Enlightenment was taking an enlightened interest in Islam and loved to read travelers' accounts of the exotic East. One of the most memorable is in Lady Mary Wortley Montagu's delightful letters, which of course Carlyle knew and admired. He wrote an appreciative encyclopedia article on her;[9] he notes that her friend "Sultan Achmed III is said to have shown a more frank disposition, and less solicitude about the Koran than usually happens."[10] She encountered, that is, a rather liberal version of Islam. Certainly she liked it and, in the Enlightenment way of finding out the great "general truths" common to all societies, discerned her own kind of Deism in Mohammedanism: "The religion of enlightened Moslems

---

6. *A Comprehensive Commentary on the Qoran, Comprising Sale's Translation and Preliminary Discourse*, ed. E. M. Wherry (Osnabrück: Otto Zeller Verlag, 1882). The life of Mahomet used by Carlyle is on pp. 68–95.

7. *Ideen, Sämtliche Werke*, vol. 14 of Suphan edition (Hildesheim: Georg Olms, 1967), pp. 426ff.

8. Quoted, DNB article on George Sale.

9. And other "M's," Montaigne, etc. s.v. "Lady Mary Wortley Montagu," *Edinburgh Encyclopedia*; *Works* 30:70–77.

10. *Works* 30:72.

was no different from the deism of sensible Christians."[11] Lady Mary, writes Bernard Lewis, was "between myths—the old one of the Muslim as barbarous infidel, the new ones of the oriental as the embodiment of mystery and romance, and, later, as the paragon of virtue, wisdom and wronged innocence."[12] The newer myth is represented in modern culture by Mozart's *Abduction from the Seraglio,* which certainly exploits the romance but delights to tweak Christian provincialism by making the supposed villain turn out to be the magnanimous Turk, whose generosity puts the Christians to shame.

Leibnitz's *Essais de théodicée* (1710) found in Islam the same "natural theology" as in Christianity, with its monotheism and its belief in immortality. Kant saw Islam, Judaism, and Christianity all as expressions of the one religion, and we have seen the lesson of tolerance that Lessing drew from this in his *Nathan der Weise.* But where Lady Mary and these *Aufklärer* were interested in Islam because it was the *same,* the new Counter-Enlightenment thinkers such as Herder and Johannes von Müller were interested in Islam because it was *different,* one of the wonderfully, infinitely variable *Vorstellungsarten.*[13] William Jones (1746–1794), who contributed much to German philology, is said to have been moved to his great language studies by delight in exotic literatures.

The French were discovering the political dimensions of Orientalism. Constantin Volney's *Voyage en Syrie et en Egypte* (1787) was useful to Napoleon. Silvestre de Sacy (1758–1838), the greatest of the French Orientalists, founded in the *Ecole royale et spéciale des langues orientales et vivantes* a tradition of sound training for the diplomatic service. He composed a famous *Chrestomathie arabe, ou*

11. Thus Robert Halsband, *The Life of Lady Mary Wortley Montagu* (New York: Oxford Univ. Press, 1956), p. 85. For her comments on Islam see *The Complete Letters of Lady Mary Wortley Montagu,* ed. Robert Halsband, 3 vols. (Oxford: Clarendon Press, 1965), especially 1:307, 318, 376.

12. *Islam in History* (London: Alcore Press, 1973), p. 38. Bernard Lewis gives a trustworthy, learned, and readable account of Orientalism in a field where one must beware of politically distorted views, especially in Edward Said's *Orientalism* (New York: Pantheon, 1978). See Bernard Lewis's corrective, "The Question of Orientalism," *New York Review of Books* 29, no. 11 (24 June 1982), 49–56. Said distorts the field shamelessly. He ignores not only the whole German school which was the most important, but also the Russians (who were indeed hostile) and Arab scholarship itself.

13. The full authoritative study is Johannes Fück, *Die Arabischen Studien in Europa* (Leipzig: Otto Harrassowitz, 1955). W. Montgomery Watt has an excellent little survey, "Carlyle on Muhammad," *The Hibbert Journal* 53 (April 1955): 247–54.

extraits de divers écrivains arabes . . . avec une traduction et des notes (Paris, 1806) and taught a whole generation of German savants, including the biblical critic Heinrich Ewald and Gustav Stickel, who first interested Goethe in things Islamic.[14] Goethe's *West-östlicher Diwan* ends with a dedication to "our master," Silvestre de Sacy.[15] Carlyle knew de Sacy and uses him, as he says, in his Mahomet lecture.[16] In England, Edward William Lane's translations of the *Thousand and One Nights* came out in monthly parts from 1838 to 1840, and Carlyle was reading them in 1839.[17] The hero of his *Wotton Reinfred* likewise reads Arabian tales and observes that they sort oddly with his mother's theological books.[18] I think it interesting that even this little touch in *Wotton Reinfred* involves the religious issue, Carlyle's "chief fact." But as everyone knows, the general enthusiasm for the Near East grew and flourished with many famous travelers, artists, and writers: Kinglake, Disraeli, Trollope, Melville, Morier, FitzGerald, Burton, Holman Hunt, Edward Lear, David Roberts; and from France, Flaubert, Hugo, Vigny, Renan, Nerval, Lamartine, Chateaubriand, Ingres.

It was the German Orientalist poets who combined the most learning with their art. Above all stands Friedrich Rückert (1788–1866), professor of Oriental languages, who did quantities of fine translations of Arabic, Persian, and Chinese verse, as well as writing fine lyric poetry of his own. In 1837 Carlyle is delighted with Rückert's translations, especially his "Hariri"; "I rejoiced over it for weeks as over a found jewel. . . . It set me searching . . . thro' Sylvestre de Sacy."[19] Hariri is the famous Arabian writer of Basra (1054–1122). Rückert translated his *Makamat* (published in 1837), the tales of a Till-Eulenspiegel-like character named Abu Seid.[20] To take up the literature of Islam is to face sooner or later questions of Comparative Religion; and then of all the great religions Islam itself is

14. Fück, p. 157.
15. *Goethes Werke* 2:267.
16. *Heroes, Works* 5:49.
17. J. A. Froude, *Thomas Carlyle: A History of His Life in London*, 2 vols. (New York: Charles Scribner's Sons, 1884; St. Clair Shores, Mich.: Scholarly Press, 1970) 1:151.
18. *Last Words of Thomas Carlyle* (London: Longmans, 1892), p. 19.
19. *Letters* 9:228, 380, 384.
20. *Die Verwandlungen des Abu Seid von Serug, oder die Makamen des Hariri*, in *Auswahl, Rückerts Werke*, herausgegeben von Georg Ellinger (Leipzig: Bibliographisches Institut, 1897), 2:281–327.

the most comparative or ecumenical and has great monuments of ecumenical thought. Both Goethe and Rückert are familiar with the Sufi poet and mystic Jalal ed-Din Rumi (1207–1273).[21] There they found a man who dedicated himself to declaring the common ground of Judeo-Christianity, Islam, and Buddhism, a mission very sympathetic to Goethe's vision of World Literature and World Religion. In Goethe's actual works, Carlyle acquired an education in Mohammedanism. Goethe tells in *Dichtung und Wahrheit* how he had read the life of Mahomet with great interest (George Sale's translation, no doubt) and spent a great deal of time and effort in 1772 and 1773 planning a play that would present Mahomet dramatically and by no means as the imposter he is in Voltaire's play, *Le Fanatisme ou Mahomet le prophète* (1741). Goethe's play remains a fragment, but out of it came a magnificent poem, "Mahomets Gesang," a kind of poeticized developmental historicism.[22] It envisions Mahomet as part of the great stream of development bearing his brothers with him to the eternal Father—the poem may have helped to shape Carlyle's worldview.

The *West-östlicher Diwan* was unquestionably one of Carlyle's source books. One of its divisions, the "Buch der Sprüche" (Book of proverbs), has a version of Carlyle's favorite scriptural text:

Noch ist der Tag, da rühre sich der Mann!
Die Nacht tritt ein, wo niemand wirken kann.

"Work while it is called Today; for the Night cometh, wherein no man can work."[23] And it has a version of the motto for *Sartor*:

Mein Erbteil wie herrlich, weit und breit!
Die Zeit ist mein Besitz, mein Acker ist die Zeit.[24]

How intimately the book shaped him is suggested by Goethe's use of

21. *Rückerts Werke* 1:39 and 308ff.; *Goethes Werke* 2:41. In German, he is usually Dschelâl-Eddîn Rumi; also called Mevlana. He founded the order of Dervishes at Konya in Turkey and composed their ritual music and a body of distinguished poetry.

22. *Goethes Werke* 1:42–44.

23. *Goethes Werke* 2:52; *Sartor*, p. 197; Ecclesiastes 9:10; John 9:4. On Carlyle's preoccupation with this text, see his little poem entitled "To-day," most readily accessible in Georg B. Tennyson's *Carlyle Reader* (New York: Random House, 1969; Cambridge: Cambridge Univ. Press, 1984), pp. 29–30.

24. *Goethes Werke* 2:52. The title page of *Sartor Resartus* has: "Mein Vermächtniss, wie herrlich weit und breit! / Die Zeit ist mein Vermächtniss, mein Acker ist die Zeit."

the word *Dialekt*, which becomes a conspicuously favorite word of
Carlyle's. Goethe appended lengthy *"Noten und Abhandlungen"*
(Notes and discussions) to the *Diwan* that present a great deal of his
Eastern lore, including Old Testament commentary. In Goethe's
discussion of "Israel in the Wilderness,"[25] C. F. Harrold finds the
source of the idea, recurrent in Carlyle's works, that in history periods
of unbelief and destruction alternate with periods of faith and
creation.[26] And then there is the passage Carlyle quotes in the lecture
on Mahomet when he explains that *Islam* means *submission to the
will of God*. "'If this be Islam,' says Goethe, 'do we not all live in
Islam?'" (5:56). In Goethe's words,

> Wenn Islam Gott ergeben heisst,
> Im Islam leben und sterben wir alle.[27]

Goethe was impatient with the insufficiency of any received religion,
finding Christianity restrictive and in part repulsive. The "submission" idea of Islam he could understand as a broad World Religion.
He was, moreover, steadfastly *naturalist*, as Arnold calls it, meaning
non-supernaturalist.[28] Mahomet eschewed miracles, as Carlyle notes
(5:68), and displayed the naturalism that for Lady Mary was the same
as the Deism of "sensible Christians." There was an added appeal for
Protestants, whether German or Scottish: Islam originated in the
reform of the idolatry into which the Judeo-Christian line was felt to
have fallen. And of the great "three" it is the broadest, the most
ecumenical—built on Judaism and accepting Jesus. The "Buch der
Parabeln" (Book of parables) in the *West-östlicher Diwan* includes a
little poem on Jesus that runs as follows:

> Jesus took down from heaven the eternal scripture of the Gospel, and read
> it night and day to his disciples; the godly word took effect. He went back
> to heaven taking it with him, and each gospeller wrote it down according
> to his own particular capacity. But as it is it's enough to keep Christians
> going right up to Judgement Day.[29]

I think this helped to form Carlyle's thought: it limits the Christian
message at the same time as it validates it. The four sets of gospel

25. "Israel in der Wüste," *Goethes Werke* 2:207ff.
26. E.g., *Sartor*, p. 19.
27. *Goethes Werke* 2:56.
28. *Collected Prose Works*, 3:10.
29. *Goethes Werke* 2:102.

clothes become, as it were, symbols of other variabilities in religions, or their *Vorstellungsarten*. No one mode is complete or absolute or final, yet all perform their indispensable function. Islam is one of them. The young Teufelsdröckh in *Sartor Resartus*, it is recorded, had read "in most Public Libraries, including those of Constantinople and Samarkand" (176); the young Carlyle, that is, exercising his German *Humanität*, does not limit his researches, for no human religion is alien to him.

Max Müller finds that it is actually in relation to Carlyle that Goethe delivers himself of some of his best statements on World Literature, which as we know subsumes religion.[30] He quotes from Goethe's introduction to the German translation of Carlyle's *Life of Schiller*, the idea of the "free intellectual commerce of the whole world." Max Müller explains how Goethe exemplified it, with the ideal of communion with the past and future and sympathy with the whole world, and with his interests in English, French, Italian, Spanish, Serbian, Bohemian, Lithuanian, Modern Greek, Swedish, Persian, Arabic, Sanskrit, and Chinese. When man acquires a reverence for the past as well as a faith in the future, he has the two combined beliefs from which "springs the first feeling of humanity in our hearts." He quotes also from Goethe's letters to Carlyle:

> We arrive best at a true toleration when we can let pass individual peculiarities . . . without quarrelling with them. . . . A translator . . . should be regarded as a trader in this great spiritual commerce. . . . The Koran says that God has given each people a prophet in his own tongue. Each translator is also a prophet to his people.[31]

And Goethe instances Luther's translation of the Bible and its immeasurable effects. Again, Goethe writes: "Herder's *Ideas* . . . have so permeated the minds of the mass of readers with us, that only a few who now read the *Ideas*, are instructed by it for the first time, for by a hundred channels and in other connections, [it] has become thoroughly familiar."[32] What had become thoroughly familiar to Goethe, and to Carlyle from reading the Germans, was Herder's great sense of

30. In an address he gave to the Goethe Society, "Goethe and Carlyle," published in *The Contemporary Review* (Philadelphia) 49, no. 294 (June 1886): 772–93.

31. "Goethe and Carlyle," p. 785; Max Müller's translation. These letters were published with somewhat different translations in *Correspondence between Goethe and Carlyle*, ed. Charles Eliot Norton (London: Macmillan, 1887).

32. *Correspondence*, p. 304; Norton's translation.

the solidarity of humanity in its shifting, endlessly varied cultures; no cultures, however different, should be alien, and we should, with understanding and sympathy, embrace even the "individual peculiarities" of religions "without quarrelling with them." This is the mission of Carlyle in the Odin and Mahomet lectures: as translator of Norse myth and of Islam he becomes a prophet to English-speaking people.

And so the second lecture of the series, "The Hero as Prophet—Mahomet," was, like the Odin lecture, an occasion of significance for the development of religious thought in English. Carlyle continues to promulgate the historicist view as he moves from paganism in the north to Mahomet among the Arabs:

> A great change; what a change and *progress* [my emphasis] is indicated here. . . ! The Hero is not now regarded as a God among his fellowmen; but as one God-inspired, as a Prophet. It is the second phasis of Hero-worship: the first or oldest, we may say, has passed away without return; in the history of the world there will not again be any man, never so great, whom his fellowmen will take for a god. (5:42)

In the spiraling cycles of development, that is, we have left the childhood of culture, when the forces of nature are experienced as anthropomorphs, and with Mahomet enter into the "heroic" age, when society takes on a hierarchical shape. Carlyle's sense of the word *prophet* is only incidentally that of someone who predicts the future but has always the primary Old Testament meaning of someone "possessed"—by God or by truth. He sees the prophet-stage as somewhere between the old-mythic-poetry stage and our new world about to come through the *palingenesia*, the Phoenix-rebirth—for which we have not yet received the New Evangel. But he feels he can point the way to it, perhaps nowhere so clearly as in these *Heroes* lectures. "Prophet" suggests to his audience the names Moses, Amos, Hosea, Isaiah, Jeremiah, John the Baptist; and he answers to that: "We have chosen Mahomet not as the most eminent Prophet; but as the one we are freest to speak of" (5:43). (How much more was this the case in his choice of Odin as god!) Mahomet "is by no means the truest of Prophets"—here Carlyle covers himself from impugning the primacy of Isaiah and the rest—"but I do esteem him a true one. Further, as there is no danger of our becoming, any of us, Mahometans, I mean to say all the good of him I justly can" (5:43). We may imagine the audience smiling at the danger of becoming Mahometans; but there *was* a certain danger. What if Richard Burton had been there? Then just at the impressionable age of nineteen, Burton later loved to play the *enfant terrible* to the Christian philistine and especially to his pious Roman Catholic wife, exclaiming how much more *moral* Islam was than hypocritical English society. Carlyle emphasizes the *progress* we have made: "It was a rude gross error, that of counting the Great Man a god" (5:42). Yes, the audience smiles at the worship of Odin; and we few note the rude gross error of understanding Jesus to be supernatural. "For . . . the Great Man, as he comes from the hand of Nature, is ever the same kind of thing: Odin [or Jesus], Luther, Johnson, Burns . . . all originally of one stuff; . . . only by the world's reception of them, and the shapes they assume, are they so immeasurably diverse" (5:43).

This is the center of the *Heroes* lectures. The rest of the lectures on poets and kings cannot be understood without this: our men of genius are the same stuff as Odin-Jesus, and our reverence for them *is* religion and is indispensable. Carlyle is the artist of the double ironic vision. Under the guise of a pretended biography he gives us in *Sartor Resartus* one of the most eloquent of autobiographies. In the Odin lecture he mediates a great deal of the new Northern mythology he had been discovering and at the same time covertly gives us a theory of the development and establishment of Christianity. Now in the Mahomet lecture he mediates a sound, sympathetic survey knowledge of Islam to a society quite ignorant of it and at the same time furthers his argument about heroes and the patterns of historical development.

As for his actual sources for the Mahomet material, he shows his familiarity with Sale, but I think he follows Johannes von Müller's *Allgemeiner Geschichten* more closely.[33] Müller's history was sympathetic to Carlyle in various ways: Müller places a large emphasis— even larger than Herder's—on *Religionsgeschichte*, religious history; he has a way of talking about an ecumenical God, a *Welt-All*, that is in Carlyle's vein; and he has a Carlylean respect for the great province of Nescience: "The human spirit, which measures the distance of the stars, which separates the presumed elements, which embraces the knowledge of the whole past, determines the destiny of millions and affects the distant future, where does it come from? Where does it go? . . . nothing seems more certain than uncertainty."[34] Müller has a sense of the worth of great men—Heroes, we could say,—such as

33. *Allgemeiner Geschichten*, 6 vols. (Stuttgart: Cottaschen Buchhandlung, 1831).
34. *Allgemeiner Geschichten* 2:95.

those who in great literature make life fuller for those who live a thousand years after them.[35] His account of Mahomet is sympathetic and full, with many specific details that Carlyle seems to borrow, such as the geographical setting of desert Bedouin culture—Carlyle's word *waste* (5:47) may echo Müller's *Wüste*.[36] In describing Mahomet as "amiable, cordial, companionable, jocose even;—a good laugh in him"—Carlyle seems to represent Müller's word *Heiterkeit*. But Müller gives him a hooked nose (*eine Nase hervorspringend*) that Carlyle withholds in describing his good looks. For some reason Carlyle withholds the Jewish connection—the Jewish mother, the Jewish support in Yathreb or Medina—although he discusses the Jewish quality of religiousness in the Arabs. Then again, his account of the brawling Christian sects (5:63) seems to echo Müller.

But though Carlyle uses various sources, his Mahomet is a consistent and lively picture full of his own loving sympathy. Mahomet's essential heroic quality is his *sincerity*, which seems to be glossed as a conviction of the religion of Wonder: "The great Fact of Existence is great to him" (5:45). He works no miracles, "yet the world, as we can see, had really from of old been all one great miracle to him" (5:68). Clearly he has faults, yet our Old Testament hero David has worse, and "David's life and history, as written for us in those Psalms of his, I consider to be the truest emblem ever given of a man's moral progress and warfare here below" (5:47). Carlyle remembers Goethe quoting the Koran to him: "They had many Prophets, these Arabs; Teachers each to his tribe, each according to the light he had"(5:48) (like Goethe's gospellers, writing each according to his capacity). But we have the "noblest of proofs" of their capacities, for scholars agree that the Book of Job comes from this region (actually from a little further East). And there follows an appreciation of Job, that favorite of his, "all men's Book"; "There is nothing written, I think, in the Bible or out of it, of equal literary merit" (5:48–49).

He refers in a scientific way to de Sacy's view that the Kaaba is an *aerolite* (5:49) (meteorite, we would say). He tells how it and the old association with Hagar's well make Mecca sacred, and how the fairs were held there, and how Christianity had reached even there: "tidings of the most important Event ever transacted in this world, the Life and

35. *Allgemeiner Geschichten* 2:96.
36. *Allgemeiner Geschichten* 3:53–58. Herder's account is much shorter: *Ideen zur Philosophie der Geschichte der Menschheit*, Suphan edition (Hildesheim: Georg Olms, 1967), 19, chap. 4, pp. 425–28.

Death of the Divine Man in Judea" (5:51). *Death* and *Man* indicate his
humanist Jesus, even though Carlyle manages to sound devout.
Having set the scene, he now proceeds with the account of Mahomet's
life. Carlyle the late-brightener notes that Mahomet was forty before
he talked of any mission. Carlyle at this time is forty-five and has only
just become a success with *The French Revolution* (1837). He marvels—as who would not?—at Mahomet's illiteracy, and yet he sees
that it frees Mahomet from "formulas and hearsays" (terms he used in
the Odin lecture): "he was alone with his own soul and the reality of
things" (5:54). He takes up the principle of Islam as submission to the
will of God; it is here that he quotes Goethe's *Diwan*: "If this be Islam,
do we not all live in Islam?" (5:56). "Islam means in its way Denial of
Self, Annihilation of Self" (5:57); this again echoes the *Diwan*: *Sterb
und werde!* (Die and come into being!).[37] On this theme Carlyle
returns to the Book of Job, quoting "Though He slay me, yet will I
trust in Him" and paraphrases the lesson of it, that man must "cease
his frantic pretension of scanning this great God's-World in his small
fraction of a brain" (5:56). He must not question but submit.

On the touching faith of the good wife Kadijah, he quotes Novalis:
"Is not Belief the true god-announcing Miracle?" (5:57)—an idea, as
we noted above, out of Hamann by Hume. And on the predictable
accusations against Mahomet, of propagating Religion by the Sword
and of condoning sensuality in Religion, he counters as best he can.
He adumbrates his sense of the relation of Might and Right not, as he
has been accused of doing, to support strong-arm governments but
rather in a sort of Darwinian way, to assert the survival of Right, as the
fittest. Milton, after all, had believed that truth would always win out
in a fair and open encounter. And then "we do not find, of the
Christian religion either, that it always disdained the sword, when
once it had got one. Charlemagne's conversion of the Saxons was not
by preaching" (5:61). The sensuality apparently sanctioned by Mahomet, he denies. Mahomet lived a frugal, not a self-indulgent, life,
and he curtailed and restricted the indulgences practiced of old.
Indulgences would not have won men to his cause. "Not by flattering
our appetites; no, by awakening the Heroic that slumbers in every
heart, can any Religion gain followers" (5:70–71). Mahomet's creed is
"a kind of Christianity" and advances as obviously beyond the chop-

37. *Goethes Werke* 2:19. The same motto is appropriated by Matthew Arnold,
Collected Prose Works 6:55–56.

logic argumentative theologies current as beyond the "rubbish of Arab idolatries" (5:63).

With the Koran, Carlyle must labor to be sympathetic. He finds it hard reading (as I do too), but it has the merit of sincerity. Yet he discovers in it gems of the religion of Wonder.

> Great clouds, he says, born in the deep bosom of the Upper Immensity, where do they come from! They hang there, the great black monsters; pour down their rain-deluges "to revive a dead earth" and grass springs, and "tall leafy palm-trees with their date clusters hanging round. Is that not a sign?" Your cattle too,—Allah made them; serviceable dumb creatures; they change the grass into milk; you have your clothing from them, very strange creatures; they come ranking home at evening-time, "and," adds he, "and are a credit to you!" . . . Miracles? cries he: What miracle would you have? Are not you yourselves there? God made *you*, "shaped you out of a little clay." Ye were small once; a few years ago ye were not at all. Ye have beauty, strength, thoughts, "ye have compassion on one another." . . . "Ye have compassion on one another"—this struck me much. (5:68–69)

It *is* a striking thing. And so is Mahomet's vision of the End:

> The whole Earth shall go spinning, whirl itself off into wreck, and as dust and vapour vanish in the Inane. Allah withdraws his hand from it, and it ceases to be. The universal empire of Allah, presence everywhere of an unspeakable Power, a Splendour, and a Terror not to be named . . . was continually clear to this man. (5:69)

And Carlyle instances Mahomet's modesty and human tenderness that show us "the genuine man, the brother of us all, brought visible through twelve centuries,—the veritable Son of our common Mother" (5:72). Islam is a great *equalizer* of men; "all men, according to Islam too, are equal; Mahomet insists not on the propriety of giving alms, but on the necessity of it. . . . The tenth part . . . is the *property* of the poor" (5:74). Islam is a discipline—and he relates this to *Wilhelm Meister's Travels* and the Master on discipline. The Mahometan heaven and hell are sensual but at the same time an *emblem* "of that grand spiritual Fact . . . the Infinite Nature of Duty" (5:75).

A kind of Christianity then, an advance on Scandinavian paganism: "Call it not false; look not at the falsehood of it, look at the truth of it. For these twelve centuries, it has been the religion and life-guidance of the fifth part of the whole kindred of Mankind. . . . To the Arab Nation it was as a birth from darkness into light; Arabia first became alive by means of it" (5:76). Nations make themselves by their culture, their religion. And this all came from one man, Mahomet. The Arabicist G. Montgomery Watt says that Carlyle's great achievement in historical context was the definitive reversal of the medieval world's picture of Islam as the great enemy. "In its essence Carlyle's conception of Muhammad is a true one, and one that is still of value in its broad outlines to the historian of today."[38] Carlyle anticipated the first modern learned and sympathetic *Life of Mahomet*, the landmark of scholarship by Gustav Weil published in 1843. Carlyle's Mahomet lecture was new; it was an education. If our modern world is not altogether ignorant and intolerant of Islam in these days when we are all closer together, some credit must go to Carlyle. *Heroes and Hero-worship* was one of the most reprinted books of the century and so "permeated the minds of readers," as Goethe said of Herder's *Ideen*, that it became such common knowledge that no one credited Carlyle with it anymore. Geoffrey Tillotson, in his valuable retrospection on Carlyle, says of the Mahomet lecture that "it stimulated if it did not create the interest in 'comparative' religion."[39] Carlyle has laid the groundwork for James Frazer, Emile Durkheim, and Mircea Eliade.

38. "Carlyle on Muhammad," p. 254.
39. *A View of Victorian Literature* (Oxford: Clarendon Press, 1978), p. 55. Tillotson also notes Carlyle's humanism: for him "men were the prime glory of the universe" (p. 63).

8. Conclusion

Carlyle's reputation through the years has suffered various vicissitudes, and from time to time even his devotees are put off by an element of rant. But he survives and is good to return to. We can scarcely understand the intellectual movements of his century without reading him; and we can understand ourselves better now in this phase of our own century by reading him. His fundamental intellectual stance is broadly satisfactory to us, and he reaches forward to us in some remarkable ways. In the preceding chapters I have outlined his role in the development of Comparative Religion, a field generally recognized as legitimate, if not basic to our thinking in these days when we are all much closer together on our planet. Carlyle intimated our modern sense of "global village": "Steam and iron," he says, "are making all the Planet into one Village."[1] And in the long perspectives of astrophysics we are much closer to each other in time as well. People not even known to Carlyle speak to us through the beautiful cave paintings of Lascaux and the touching Epic of Gilgamish; and we send their messages forward in the time capsules of innumerable printed books.

Just as Carlyle found his way out of the parochialism of Christianity into the wider world of multiplicities of mythmaking, where the many varied forms of religion are the most important and characteristic products of humankind, so he also found his way out of other dogmatisms and other parochialisms into a vision of an infinite universe and infinite possibilities. The movement from Christianity into Comparative Religion offers a model for the nineteenth-century movement of mind, what Nelson Goodman sees as

that mainstream of modern philosophy that began when Kant exchanged

---

1. *Correspondence of Carlyle and Emerson* (New York, 1883/1886), quoted by Geoffrey Tillotson, *A View of Victorian Literature* (Oxford: Clarendon Press, 1978), 1:207.

the structure of the world for the structure of the mind, continued when C. I. Lewis exchanged the structure of the mind for the structure of concepts, and that now proceeds to exchange the structure of concepts for the structure of the several symbol systems of sciences, philosophy, the arts, perception and everyday discourse. The movement is from unique truth and a world fixed and found to a diversity of right and even conflicting versions or worlds in the making.[2]

Carlyle's sense of the structure of mind is very clear in his consistent analyses of language as multiform and provisional, temporary mutable *clothes* as in the Herderian expressivist vision. Languages make our "worlds." The variable *clothes* of culture in *Sartor* are most often the "visible Garment for that divine ME . . . cast hither like a light-particle, down from Heaven." But when Carlyle comes to language, it seems rather to be that by which we exist: "Language is called the Garment of Thought: however, it should rather be, Language is the Flesh-Garment, the Body, of Thought. I said that imagination wove this Flesh-Garment; and does not she? Metaphors are her stuff."[3] God, the devil, hell, are linguistic inventions that reify in images the felt experience of a society. They are the Ancient Dialect of unconscious metaphor. When we recognize them as metaphorical, we do not thereby invalidate them but see them as part of the invaluable human tradition of religious myth, or "poetry." Jupiter, Odin, Jehovah can all coexist for us now.

Mikhail Bakhtin is gaining recognition as an important modern witness of the movement from the one to the many, and his understanding of the "dialogic imagination" answers well to our multiplicities and pluralisms. He starts, as Carlyle starts, from the idea of man as constitutionally social. "It is in Society," says Carlyle, "that man first feels what he is, first becomes what he can be."[4] And his good is to be found in standing "encompassed, and spiritually embraced, by a cloud of witnesses and brothers, . . . [in the] living literal *Communion of Saints*, wide as the World itself, and as the History of the World."[5] In a consonant way, Bakhtin insists that

2. Quoted in part, above, chapter 2. Nelson Goodman, *Ways of Worldmaking* (Indianapolis: Hackett Publishing Co., 1978), p. x. With thanks to Virgil Nemoianu for directing attention to this book in his article, "Under the Sign of Leibniz: The Growth of Aesthetic Power," *New Literary History* 16, no. 3 (Spring 1985): 609–25.

3. *Sartor*, p. 73.

4. "Characteristics," *Works* 28:10.

5. *Sartor*, p. 247.

the interhuman is the foundation of the human. To be . . . means to communicate, and we are all caught up in relations of dialogue, not only with those to whom we speak in the present, but also with those in the future, whose replies we anticipate and internalize, and those of the past, whose voices come to us through our language and culture.[6]

Democracy the many-voiced has its risks, as Carlyle so well knows; but the dogma of the single-voiced Marxist state is worse, and Bakhtin himself was a noble martyr to it.[7] "Literature is our Parliament," says Carlyle.

> Printing, which comes necessarily out of Writing, I say often, is equivalent to Democracy: invent writing, Democracy is inevitable. Writing brings Printing; brings universal everyday extempore Printing, as we see at present. Whoever can speak, speaking now to the whole nation, becomes a power, a branch of government, with inalienable weight in law-making, in all acts of authority. It matters not what rank he has, what revenues or garnitures: the requisite thing is, that he have a tongue which others will listen to; this and nothing more is requisite. The nation is governed by all that has tongue in the nation: Democracy is virtually *there.*[8]

The dialogic imagination itself comes to Carlyle's aid to solve his most pressing literary problem in the triumphant scheme of *Sartor,* built upon a pluralism of voices, chiefly Teufelsdröckh's and the Editor's. He continues to exploit voices: in *The French Revolution* he creates whole phalanxes of varied points of view, and in other works an imaginative *dramatis personae* of Plugson of Undershot, Sir Jabesh Windbag, Sauerteig, the Irish Widow, and the rest. And what else are his literary studies and his histories but essays to determine distinctive voices? The proper study of mankind for him is not man but rather men, in their variety and individuation, the miracle of miracles, the true Shekinah, the Hero.[9]

His work constituted a deliverance for innumerable contemporaries. George Eliot's well-known judgment may be quoted once more

---

6. This is from a summary of the essential Bakhtin by Tzvetan Todorov, *Times Literary Supplement* (14 June 1985): 675.

7. Katerina Clark and Michael Holquist reveal the political context of Bakhtin's criticism, and its touching relevance to his criticism, in their *Mikhail Bakhtin* (Cambridge, Mass.: Harvard Univ. Press, 1984).

8. *Heroes, Works* 5:164.

9. Albert J. LaValley rightly recognizes "awareness of multiplicity" as one of the central Carlylean concerns in *Carlyle and the Idea of the Modern* (New Haven: Yale Univ. Press, 1968), p. 11.

here: "There is hardly a superior or active mind of this generation that has not been modified by Carlyle's writing."[10] He was in tune with contemporary science. It is true that he appears hostile to Darwin, even Darwin who himself confesses to something like Carlylean "wonder" at the marvels of evolution. I think it is actually the reductive *effect* of popular Darwinism that Carlyle deplores; certainly the main line of evolutionary thought is very like what he espouses in Herder's *Entwicklung*. And his Might-is-Right doctrine, mistakenly understood as proto-Nazi, is in fact a Darwinian evolutionary idea, the survival of the *morally* fittest, a natural selection in ethics; it represents Carlyle's ultimate faith in the decency of humankind.

Huxley, "Darwin's bulldog," revered Carlyle. He tells how he emerged from darkness to "better things."

> And when I look back, what do I find to have been agents of my redemption? The hope of immortality or of future reward? I can honestly say that for fourteen years such a consideration has never entered my head. No, I can tell you exactly what has been at work. *Sartor Resartus* led me to know that a deep sense of religion was compatible with the entire absence of theology.[11]

Frank M. Turner surveys Carlyle's relationship to Victorian science and illuminates Huxley's view. Carlyle opened a way, says Turner, for scientists "to regard themselves as thoroughly scientific and naturalistic without becoming either materialistic or atheistic. . . . In this respect Carlyle's idealist concepts and moral doctrines eased the transition from a religious apprehension of the universe to a scientific and secular one."[12] For Carlyle, we might add, the scientific apprehension of the universe is the religious one. Turner observes that

> Natural Supernaturalism, by asserting the grandeur and marvel of nature in the face of the absence of miracles, the limitations of human knowledge, and the ultimate mystery of things, provided the secular equivalent of a spiritual sanction to activity in this world. . . . Huxley could write that the doctrine of immortality "is not half so wonderful as the conservation of

10. Reviewing anonymously Thomas Ballantyne's *Passages Selected from the Writings of Carlyle* in the *Leader* (27 October 1855); quoted in *Thomas Carlyle: The Critical Heritage*, ed. Jules Paul Seigel (London: Routledge and Kegan Paul, 1971), p. 410.

11. Quoted by Noel Annan, *Leslie Stephen, the Godless Victorian* (New York: Random House, 1984), p. 240.

12. Frank M. Turner, "Scientific Naturalism and Carlyle," *Victorian Studies* 18, no. 3 (March 1975): 330.

force, or the indestructibility of matter" . . . and Tyndall . . . "It is the function of science, not as some think to divest this universe of its wonder and mystery, but . . . to point out the wonder and the mystery of common things."[13]

From personal experience Tyndall describes Carlyle's informed understanding and passionate interest in contemporary science. He acclaims the accuracy of the metaphors Carlyle frequently derived from science and tells how he grasped "the principle of Continuity, and saw the interdependence of 'parts' in the 'stupendous Whole.'" In passages of *Sartor* Carlyle "foreshadows the doctrine of the Conservation of Energy": "Detached, separated! I say there is no such separation; nothing hitherto was ever stranded, cast aside; but all, were it only a withered leaf, works together with all, and lives through perpetual metamorphoses."[14]

Still more interesting on the degree of orthodoxy of Carlyle's religion, Tyndall records a conversation. As they were making a walking excursion in the New Forest, Carlyle complained of the collapse of religious feeling in England. Tyndall said to him: "'As regards the most earnest and the most capable of the men of a generation younger than your own, if one writer more than another has been influential in loosing them from their theological moorings, thou art the man!'"[15] Tyndall records no demurrer. No doubt Carlyle was sufficiently aware of Tyndall as one of the faithful in the religion of wonder. What ensued in the conversation was a mutual agreement that it was a great advance to have abolished hellfire,[16] and Carlyle told how cruelly his father had suffered from the doctrine. "It surely is a great gain to have abolished this Terror."[17]

Finally, Tyndall writes pointedly on Carlyle's worldview. For himself as for Carlyle, he writes:

> After science has completed her mission upon earth, the finite known will still be embraced by the infinite unknown. And this "boundless contiguity of shade," by which our knowledge is hemmed in, will always tempt the exercise of belief and imagination. The human mind, in its structural and

13. "Scientific Naturalism and Carlyle," 337–38.
14. John Tyndall, *New Fragments* (New York: Appleton, 1892), pp. 385–86.
15. *New Fragments*, p. 376.
16. In the 1860 heresy trials of the writers of *Essays and Reviews*, the Privy Council found that Eternity of Torment, as embodied in the Athanasian Creed, was not essential doctrine. Many clergymen were loath to give it up.
17. *New Fragments*, p. 377.

poetic capacity, can never be prevented from building its castles—on the rock or in the air, as the case may be—in this ultrascientific region. Certainly the mind of Carlyle could not have been prevented from doing so. Out of pure Unintelligence he held that Intelligence never could have sprung, and so, at the heart of things, he placed an Intelligence—an Energy which, "to avoid circuitous periphrasis, we call God." I am here repeating his own words to myself. Every reader of his works will have recognized the burning intensity of his conviction that this universe is ruled by veracity and justice, which are sure in the end to scorch and dissipate all falsehood and wrong.[18]

Such is the extent of Carlyle's supernaturalism, and such is his sense of the Ancient Dialect: minimally, it "avoids circuitous periphrasis."

And such was his sympathy with Victorian science. Still more remarkable is his sympathy with the course of science today. Einstein's famous dictum indicates the contemporary situation: "As the circumference of light increases so does the edge of darkness." It constitutes, in a kind of algebraic progression, an endorsement of the Carlylean respect for *Nescience* and the "religion of wonder." From outposts all along that circumference come the corroborations. Alan Sandage speaks about creation: "As astronomers, you can't say anything except here is a miracle. . . . an incredible mystery: Why is there something instead of nothing?"[19] We can refer again to Einstein: "What is there about the human mind that so resonates with the rest of the universe that we're able to understand anything about the workings of nature on the largest scale?"[20]

In 1835 in Ecclefechan, Carlyle spied Halley's comet and wrote to John Stuart Mill about it: "The wonder hung himself out gratuitously for me . . . hurrying on, with high-pressure and speed, God knows whence, God knows whither, and on what business! . . . who could but say to him: Hail, thou brother Thing!"[21] Here is Alan Sandage: "Every single atom in your body was once inside a star. We are all brothers in that sense."[22] Or Primo Levi on the atom of carbon that has flown around the world, through a flower, and into a nerve cell in his brain: "The atom is in my writing; it guides this hand of mine to

18. *New Fragments*, pp. 395–96.

19. He is speaking on the TV Special, *The Creation of the Universe*, 20 November 1985; the text was written and presented by Timothy Ferris (Kent, Ohio: PTV Publications, 1985); p. 15.

20. Quoted by Ferris, p. 18.

21. *Letters* 8:250.

22. Quoted by Ferris, p. 2.

impress upon the paper this dot, here, this one."[23] Carlyle's "Organic Filaments" at work with a vengeance! Often in *Sartor* Carlyle writes in Kantian terms of the mystery of Space and Time as "thought-forms," and we have yet to cancel out this mystery. "It may be," says physicist Stephen Hawking, "that spacetime forms a closed surface without an edge, rather like the surface of the Earth, but in two more dimensions."[24] The mind boggles. Which seems to be our way of saying we recognize our mental limitations. It happens not only in astrophysics and chemistry but also in physiology, in brain research, in linguistic research, in entomology, in the study of bird migrations. All round the circumference each discovery seems more astounding than the last, and each by no means settles the matter but rather opens up an array of new questions, new mysteries. There is the psychologist who declares he never could interest himself in extrasensory perception because the processes of perception itself are so staggering, so "marvelous." There is Noam Chomsky, taking language as a "central aspect" of human intelligence, declaring recurrently that the human mind may not be up to understanding how the human mind works.[25] Nescience is sometimes quantified, although Carlyle insisted upon its infinity. We are told that astronomers, from the ancients observing at Stonehenge to the latest launchers of a space telescope, have studied only about a tenth of all the matter in the universe. But then if, as some suppose, "dark matter is made up of black holes, it would be a mystery cloaked in an enigma."[26] Carlyle is a poet for our world, and a poet for scientists.

But this is not to say that he would give license to mystery-mongering. We must remember the rigor of his early training in mathematics, a phase of his career that has seldom been particularly connected with his writings.[27] But it does connect. At a stage of

23. The chapter "Carbon" in Primo Levi's *The Periodic Table*, trans. R. Rosenthal (New York: Schocken, 1984).

24. Quoted by Ferris, p. 15.

25. See my "Waiting for Gödel: Some Literary Examples of Hierarchical Thinking," in *Language, Logic, and Genre*, ed. Wallace Martin (Lewisburg, Pa.: Bucknell Univ. Press, 1974), pp. 29–30.

26. Betty Ann Kevles, "Shedding Light on Dark Matter," *Los Angeles Times*, 8 September 1983.

27. Carlisle Moore has a fine study of Carlyle's mathematics and its place in his career ("Carlyle: Mathematics and 'Mathesis,'" in *Carlyle Past and Present*, ed. K. J. Fielding and Rodger L. Tarr [New York: Barnes and Noble, 1976], pp. 61–95). He notes Carlyle's sympathy for Pascal (one of his early encyclopedia subjects) and Pascal's embodiment of the relationship of math and religion; he acclaims the essay on proportion as "a model of concision" and proposes that this essay "into the realm of

phenomenal intellectual growth, mathematics absorbed, developed, and sustained him. Cast like Bertrand Russell into a sea of relativity, he found a stability in mathematics, seeking, in Russell's words, "to apprehend the Pythagorean power by which number holds sway above the flux, . . . an ideal world where everything is perfect and yet true."[28] When Carlyle was in Edinburgh, the only teacher he really respected was the mathematician John Leslie, whose favorite pupil he was. For a time "geometry shone before me as the noblest of all sciences, and I prosecuted it in all my best hours and moods."[29] He provided Leslie with a geometric solution of the real roots of any quadratic equation, which Leslie published in the third edition (1817) of his *Elements of Geometry*. We are told by a modern mathematician that it is "remarkable in its originality, beautiful in its simplicity."[30] For his own translation of Legendre's *Eléments de géométrie* (1828), Carlyle wrote a prefatory essay on proportion that might be viewed as part of the nineteenth century's address to the *relative* rather than the absolute. This century also saw the development of differential calculus to cope with the instability of things. The most famous English mathematician of the day, Augustus de Morgan, commended Carlyle's essay on proportion. It was incorporated into Brewster's *Geometry*, a textbook that completely supplanted Euclid in America and so subtly influenced a whole generation of the New World.[31]

I think it can be said that the rigor and energy of Carlyle's mathematical thinking went toward shaping his worldview; it helped him to recognize in Goethe the main solution to the conflict between religion and science and to draw the borderline between science and nescience. Mathematics as metaphor runs revealingly through all his works. The famous injunction to lessen one's denominator rather than increase one's numerator is one example among many.[32] A mathematical understanding of the world is his basis. "Which of your philosoph-

approximation and incommensurabilities has a special significance" in the light of Carlyle's later work and his tendency to "intuitive, analogical thinking." "His mathematical habits . . . continued in force to determine [his] special mode of thinking, arguing and proving" (pp. 78, 80, 81, 90).

28. Bertrand Russell, *The Autobiography* (Boston: Little Brown and Co., 1951), pp. 4, 254.

29. *Two Reminiscences of Thomas Carlyle*, ed. John Clubbe (Durham: Duke Univ. Press, 1974), p. 36.

30. Peter A. Wursthorn, "The Position of Thomas Carlyle in the History of Mathematics," *The Mathematics Teacher* (December 1966): 756.

31. "The Position of Thomas Carlyle," 769.

32. *Sartor*, p. 191.

ical systems is other than a dream-theorem; a net quotient, confidently given out where divisor and dividend are both unknown!"[33]

Again and again in his writings he arrives at things known now in mathematics as "limitation results." It is as a brilliantly conceived corollary to the epistemological problem that he writes in 1831 in "Characteristics,"

> Metaphysics is the attempt of the mind to rise above the mind; to environ and shut in, or as we say, *comprehend* the mind. Hopeless struggle . . . ! What strength of sinew, or athletic skill, will enable the stoutest athlete to fold his own body in his arms, and, by lifting, lift up *himself*? The Irish Saint swam the Channel "carrying his head in his teeth"; but the feat has never been imitated.[34]

The precise mathematical demonstration of this situation had to await Kurt Gödel's proof in 1931 of the now famous theorem. Logical systems are not self-justifying. To prove such a system as mathematics free from potential contradiction, one must use principles outside mathematics; and then to prove that these new principles do not conceal contradictions, one must use new principles beyond them. The regress has no end—one has languages and metalanguages without limit.[35] "What theorem of the Infinite can the Finite render complete?" asks Carlyle.[36] "Nature remains of quite *infinite* depth, of quite *infinite* expansion. . . . The course of Nature's phases, on this our little fraction of a Planet, is partially known to us: but who knows what deeper courses these depend on; what infinitely larger cycle (of causes) our like Epicycle revolves on?"[37]

The insufficiency of our knowledge and our language is Carlyle's recurrent theme, and he habitually envisages hierarchy. Even "Universal History is but a sort of Parish History; which the 'P. P. Clerk of this Parish,' member of 'our Alehouse Club' . . . puts together,—in such sort as his fellow-members will praise."[38] The homeliness of the

---

33. *Sartor*, p. 54.
34. *Essays* 3:27.
35. P. W. Bridgman, *The Way Things Are* (Cambridge, Mass.: Harvard Univ. Press, 1959), p. 6. In a study I did some years ago on some literary analogues to Gödel's theorem, I brought in an Eastern religious dictum by way of Alan Watts: "Trying to define yourself is like trying to bite your own teeth" ("Waiting for Gödel," in *Language, Logic, and Genre*, pp. 28–44). Carlyle's Irish saint is similarly apposite and rather more amusing.
36. "Characteristics," *Essays* 3:25.
37. *Sartor*, pp. 257–58.
38. "On History Again," *Essays* 3:165.

village alehouse club addresses our littleness with humor and compassion. Sometimes the rhetoric is indignant: on the arrogance of man in believing himself capable of a proof of God, he urges him "to cease his frantic pretension of scanning this great God's-World in his small fraction of a brain."[39] Or the pretension is absurd: "*Proof* of a God? A *probable* God! The smallest of Finites struggling to *prove* to itself, that is . . . to picture-out and arrange as diagram, and *include* within itself, the Highest Infinite!"[40]

It happens that the literary locus classicus of limitation results and of Gödel's theorem is Carlyle's favorite literary work. This is the biblical Book of Job, which consistently informs his thought early and late. "There is nothing written, I think, in the Bible or out of it, of equal literary merit. . . . It is our first, oldest statement of the never-ending Problem,—man's destiny, and God's ways with him here in this earth. . . . Sublime sorrow, sublime reconciliation; oldest choral melody as of the heart of mankind."[41] There is good reason to take seriously this evaluation of the Book of Job and to note its placement within the undifferentiated continuum of literature-scripture, the tradition of hero-writers, the communion of secular saints. It is perhaps unique among scriptures in that it bears practically no sectarian stamp; and given the framework tale as frankly fiction—the most literalist interpreters would be hard put to claim otherwise—there is nothing in it that is not in accord with the scientific mind. It presents the classic test case, the best of men faced with the greatest adversity. The folktale framework guarantees the reader's superior, informed position; as we see Job stricken and attend to the discourses of Job and the comforters, presenting samples of the ways in which we try to rationalize the problem of suffering, we know more than the actors themselves. The poet exploits the naiveté of the folktale: of course we know this is not the way things are, a sort of informal reception in heaven and affable discussion between the Prince of Darkness and the Unknowable; since we cannot know the way things are—as the whole poem asserts—this banal fairy tale or myth or legend suggests how we must make do with provisional epistemologies. These may be heuristic fictions, the means to otherwise unattainable insights that are themselves valid. Even though banal, then, the framework affords us the detached ironic perspective, and

39. *Heroes, Works* 5:56.
40. "Diderot," *Essays* 3:231.
41. *Heroes, Works* 5:49.

we are by suggestion already *outside the system* of formal logic functioning in the dialogues.

The formal logic of the dialogues is not naive or banal. The contradictions, the paradoxes, the anomalies of this *system* of intellectualizing man's predicament are made cumulatively more obvious and painful, till the poet makes a great and memorable shift in perspective and takes us out of that intellectual system into a metasystem.

> Who is this that darkeneth counsel by words without knowledge? Gird up now thy loins like a man; for I will demand of thee, and answer thou me. Where wast thou when I laid the foundations of the earth? declare, if thou hast understanding. Who hath laid the measures thereof, if thou knowest? or who hath stretched the line upon it? Whereupon are the foundations thereof fastened? or who laid the corner stone thereof; when the morning stars sang together, and all the sons of God shouted for joy? (38:2–7)

The metasystem is demonstrated, the ineffable is presented, by way of symbol. The syntax itself, all unanswerable question now, symbolizes the departure from discursive logic. We are reminded of Wittgenstein's assertion "Unsayable things do indeed exist" (*Tractatus* 6:522) and the severe last proposition of the *Tractatus*: "Whereof one cannot speak, thereof one must be silent." Compare Job now: "I will lay mine hand upon my mouth" (40:4). So must the arithmetician, says Gödel, lay his hand upon his mouth at a certain point. At a similar point Carlyle recommends Silence over Speech.[42]

Commentators on Gödel's theorem warn that it "should not be rashly called upon to establish the primacy of some act of intuition that would dispense with formalization."[43] True. Mathematicians still have a discipline. One of the most moving things about the Book of Job is that it reserves dignity and integrity to man's intellect. "Though he slay me, yet . . . I will maintain my own ways before him." Neither the comforters nor the universe can bully him into saying what he knows is *not true*.

What solace is here for the sufferer from Wotton's Complaint! "His love of truth . . . had ruined him; yet he would not relinquish the search to whatever abysses it might lead."[44]

---

42. *Sartor*, p. 219.
43. *The Way Things Are*, p. 7.
44. *Wotton Reinfred*, in *Last Words of Thomas Carlyle* (London: Longmans, 1892), p. 28.

What can it profit any mortal to adopt locutions and imaginations which do *not* correspond to fact; which no sane mortal can deliberately adopt in his soul as true; which the most orthodox of mortals can only, and this after infinite essentially *impious* effort to put-out the eyes of his mind, persuade himself to "believe that he believes"?[45]

The relief comes with Goethe's *Entsagen*, the renouncement of dogma and certainty, and the realization that the dogmatist is insufferably arrogant in claiming knowledge of what he cannot know. The poetic unanswerable questions from the Whirlwind symbolize the limits of knowledge and symbolize also a cosmos infinitely more wonderful than anything a theology can present. We must be wary of conventional commentary on the Book of Job, for that is the work of those who have a professional investment in theology. We need the uncommitted, disinterested interpreter. "The book is not a philosophical theodicy but rather a protest against any such thing," says Theodore Gaster.[46] David Daiches writes:

> The only answer to Job's question is that there is no answer: the universe is more complicated than man can ever hope to understand. . . . Yet Job is not punished for having raised the question; instead, his friends are reproved for having given the neat, conventional answers.[47]

God's reply emphasizes the mystery and the paradox. Man must recognize them, but he must accept that he cannot fathom them. The solution to Job's problem, in fact, is subsumed in *wonder*.[48]

Carlyle's chapter "Natural Supernaturalism" is the part of *Sartor* that presents the new religion, and in it are to be found the greatest number of allusions to and echoes of the Book of Job—as might be expected, for the Book of Job is the scripture of Carlyle's religion of Wonder. "Custom," says Professor Teufelsdröckh,

> doth make dotards of us all. . . . Philosophy complains that Custom has hoodwinked us, from the first; that we do everything by Custom, even Believe by it; that our very Axioms, let us boast of Free-thinking as we may, are oftenest simply such Beliefs as we have never heard questioned. Nay, what is Philosophy throughout but a continual battle against Cus-

45. *Life of Sterling*, *Works* 11:51. Quoted above in chapter 5.
46. Theodore H. Gaster, *Myth, Legend, and Custom in the Old Testament* (New York: Harper and Row, 1969), p. 784.
47. David Daiches, "The Book of Job," in *More Literary Essays* (Chicago: Univ. of Chicago Press, 1956), p. 271.
48. David Daiches, *God and the Poets* (Oxford: Clarendon Press, 1984), p. 25.

tom. . . ? Am I to view the Stupendous with stupid indifference, because I
have seen it twice, or two-hundred, or two-million times?[49]

The Professor takes up the question of miracles and finds them a
relative matter. To the king of Siam, an icicle would be a miracle. But
God and his laws must be unalterable. But—here at the center of
Sartor Resartus is the argument from Job: What must those unalterable rules be?

> They stand written in our Works of Science, say you; in the accumulated
> records of Man's Experience?—was Man with his Experience present at
> the Creation, then, to see how it all went on? Have any deepest Scientific
> individuals yet dived down to the foundations of the Universe, and gauged
> everything there? Did the Maker take them into His counsel?[50]

The questions continue as in Job—unanswerable, humbling, awe-
inspiring questions that insist on man's Nescience and on the mystery
and grandeur of creation. We are so used to them that we cannot see
them.

And Carlyle sees it as the work of "Philosophy"—or Religion-
Literature—to combat blind Custom and open our eyes to Wonder.
In our century there has developed an aesthetic analogous to this; I
mean the theory formulated by Victor Shklovsky as *ostranenija*,
making strange, or defamiliarization. "People living at the seashore,"
writes Shklovsky, "grow so accustomed to the murmur of the waves
that they never hear it. By the same token, we scarcely even hear the
words which we utter. . . . We look at each other, but we do not see
each other anymore. Our perception of the world has withered
away."[51] It is this dotage that the artist is called upon to counteract. By
taking the object out of its habitual context, he gives us a heightened
awareness. "Art exists that one may recover the sensation of life; it
exists to make one feel things, to make the stone stony."[52] And this,
we may add, is just how the Whirlwind chapters of Job function. For
Carlyle the function was a religious one.

Some of Carlyle's contemporaries were thinking along the same
lines. Wordsworth sees that poetry functions "to throw . . . a certain

49. *Sartor*, p. 259.

50. *Sartor*, p. 256.

51. Quoted in Victor Erlich, *Russian Formalism*, 2d rev. ed. (The Hague: Mouton
and Co., 1965), pp. 176–77.

52. Victor Shklovsky, in *Russian Formalist Criticism: Four Essays*, trans. Lee T.
Lemon and Marion J. Reis (Lincoln: Univ. of Nebraska Press, 1965), p. 12.

colouring of imagination, whereby ordinary things should be presented to the mind in an unusual way."[53] But Wordsworth sees Nature and the mind of man as beautifully adapted to one another; Carlyle sees the mind of man as hopelessly inadequate to comprehend Nature. Coleridge sees the power of genius "to carry on the feelings of childhood into the powers of manhood; to combine the child's sense of wonder and novelty with the appearances, which every day for perhaps fifty years had rendered familiar . . . , to awaken the mind's attention from the lethargy of custom."[54] Coleridge, however, wanted Christianity and a church—the Anglican church—as well. For Carlyle, Wonder is enough.

In John Holloway's ground-breaking study of Carlyle in *The Victorian Sage*, still one of the best, and the only one to take up at any length Carlyle's use of the Bible, Carlyle is presented as one of the lay-preachers who fill an emotional need for those to whom orthodox religion has become untenable.[55] Holloway sees biblical language as a device by which Carlyle becomes the preacher. "Actually, by using this Biblical language and at the same time often sharply criticizing conventional religion, Carlyle gets the best of both worlds."[56] True in a way; but it suggests a Carlyle more calculating and duplicitous than he was. The Book of Job itself criticizes conventional religion. And it was as natural to Carlyle to use the biblical idiom as to use that of Shakespeare or Goethe, and he used them all in his densely allusive style without compunction, as they served him. He would say of Christianity what Thor said to King Olaf in his last appearance: "Have a care"—lest you throw out the literature with the dogma. Speaking of Dante, he had said the poetry will outlive the religion. Carlyle himself would stand "ever encompassed, and spiritually embraced, by a cloud of witnesses and brothers" in what he called the "living literal [though he means *figurative*] Communion of Saints, wide as the World itself, and as the History of the World."[57] Christianity would be for Carlyle, as it was for Goethe, constrictive. He himself appropriated Goethe's world culture, and he extended English-speaking culture immeasurably.

Carlyle as I have presented him in this study is far from complete;

53. 1802 Preface to *Lyrical Ballads*.
54. *Biographia Literaria*, Engell-Bate edition, 1:ii, 80–81.
55. *The Victorian Sage* (London: Macmillan, 1953).
56. *The Victorian Sage*, p. 24.
57. *Sartor*, p. 247.

in this open-minded modernist, one may miss the old prophetic ranter. The English, said Emerson with rather mischievous glee, "keep Carlyle as a sort of portable cathedral bell." In his "Sage of Chelsea" days, any important issue would be brought before him and he would emit grand and holy sounds, often dogmatic sounds. And with reference to God Carlyle would often lay down a line that sounds like old-fashioned orthodoxy; one might wish he had indulged himself more in his old "sacred silences." But even when he sounds most orthodox, I believe he felt safely covered by his old theory of metaphor and allowed himself to use the Ancient Dialect with impunity. For Carlyle, as for other Victorians, system and consistency were in bad odor. Bentham had been wonderfully systematic and, as all the great Victorians would agree, wonderfully inadequate. Bentham gave consistency a bad name. Carlyle scorned it. Arnold did not, I think, strive for it unduly. Ruskin is outrageously inconsistent, without compunction. Trollope, I have argued elsewhere, elaborately avoids the *parti pris*. But Carlyle had taken on the prophetic office and acquired the habit of laying down the law—and we ask consistency from prophets. The ground of his attitudes was unchanging. The depth of his human sympathy and pity is proportionate to his outrage and exasperation. His heart sick and sore for his generation, heavy-burdened, he leans on his essential insight that human problems cannot all be solved by scientific progress and democracy. And from that insight, once shared, we cannot retrograde.

The German Wilhelm Dilthey, more or less the father of *Geistesgeschichte*, history of ideas, and well known for his emphasis on religious culture, is an especially appropriate assessor of Carlyle. Dilthey sees Carlyle as being in the nineteenth century what Voltaire was in his time, a key figure.[58] Carlyle found (I paraphrase Dilthey) in German thought the intellectual wherewithal to confront Enlightenment positivism, a scientifically feasible answer to a falsely reductive "science." He gave it an effective form that made it a force in the nation and—Dilthey implies—beyond. It is Dilthey's judgment that he was the greatest English writer of his century and an informing element of European culture.

Of all the wonders of creation to which he would open our eyes, man is the most wonderful. Anyone who studies and knows the achievements of great artists in music or painting or poetry will

58. "Thomas Carlyle," *Archiv für Geschichte der Philosophie* 4 (1891): 260–85.

understand. In the face of the whole creation challenging man's infinite mind, infinitely, who needs miracles? No limit has ever been set. The sense of human capacity as the greatest of wonders is the essence of Weimar humanism and it is Carlyle's religion. It is the doctrine of *Heroes and Hero-worship*, in which God and prophet are proper metaphors. *"We* are the miracle of miracles."[59]

59. *Heroes, Works* 5:10.

Index

Compositor: Harrington-Young Typography and Design
Text: 10/12 Sabon
Display: Sabon
Printer: Braun-Brumfield
Binder: Braun-Brumfield